FROM NYET
TO DA

FROM NYET TO DA

UNDERSTANDING THE NEW RUSSIA

Fourth Edition

YALE RICHMOND

INTERCULTURAL PRESS
A Nicholas Brealey Publishing Company

BOSTON • LONDON

First published by Intercultural Press, a division of Nicholas Brealey
Publishing, in 1992. Revised in 1996, 2003, and 2009.

Nicholas Brealey Publishing
20 Park Plaza, Suite 1115A
Boston, MA 02116, USA
Tel: + 617-523-3801
Fax: + 617-523-3708
www.interculturalpress.com

Nicholas Brealey Publishing
3-5 Spafield Street, Clerkenwell
London, EC1R 4QB, UK
Tel: +44-(0)-207-239-0360
Fax: +44-(0)-207-239-0370
www.nicholasbrealey.com

Printed in the United States of America

13   12   11   10   09   1   2   3   4   5

ISBN: 978-1-931930-59-8

Library of Congress Cataloging-in-Publication Data
Richmond, Yale.
  From nyet to da : understanding the new Russia / Yale Richmond. —4th
ed.
     p. cm.
  Includes bibliographical references and index.
  1. Russia (Federation)   2. National characteristics, Russian.
3. Social psychology—Russia (Federation)   4. Russia (Federation)—
Social life and customs.   I. Title.
  DK510.23.R53 2009
  947.085—dc22

2008033880

To all who want to know more about the new Russia and the opportunities there for business, scholarly and scientific work, or tourism—and how the new Russia resembles the old Russia.

CONTENTS

Contents

Contents

I have never met anyone who understood Russians.

—Grand Duke Aleksandr Mikhailovich Romanov (1866–1933)

In the last five years, everything has changed. In the last 200 years, nothing has changed.

—New Russian saying

The new Russia . . . a bewildering mix of capitalism, corruption, mob violence, political consultants, policemen who are hired killers, feminism, Chechen terrorists and, most incredibly, nostalgia for Joe Stalin.

—Patrick Anderson, in *The Washington Post*, June 12, 2007

xii

PREFACE TO THE FOURTH EDITION

T HE COLD WAR IS A THING OF THE PAST, commu-
nism has collapsed, and Russia has experienced extraordinary
changes. Its relations with the West have broadened. A new middle class is
emerging. Russians are traveling abroad freely and have access to the Internet. Vladimir Putin has come and stayed. Foreign visitors are finding Russia a more pleasant place to visit. But Russia, nevertheless, remains distant,
separated from the West by culture, language, and history. As U.S. Secretary
of State Condoleezza Rice described the U.S.-Russian relationship in 2007,
it is one of "cooperation and competition, and friendship and friction."[1] And,
I would add, "and mystery and misunderstanding" as the West learned
when Russia invaded neighboring Georgia in August 2008.

Though no longer a superpower, Russia is still a great power with
which the West must seek cooperation on numerous issues ranging from
terrorism to arms control. Russia, for its part, needs foreign investment and
Western know-how. Joint ventures find willing partners, but doing business
with the Russians can still be burdensome as long-held patterns of behavior
continue to be influenced by geography, history, and culture. Understanding
the Russians—the theme of this book—continues to remain a challenge.

This edition has been revised and updated to cover events and changes
occurring in Russia since the third edition was published in 2003. Russia is
indeed changing, but most of the Russians whom foreign visitors may
encounter will still show many of the traits described here and in earlier editions. Differences may be seen between city dwellers and rural people, the
intelligentsia and workers and peasants, and between generations, but they all
share many common characteristics, which will be described in these pages.

There are no shortcuts to understanding the Russians or avoiding the
friction foreseen by Secretary Rice, but it helps to know their language, history, and literature and to have worked with them over the years. Although

not intended as a quick fix, this book has been written for readers without previous experience in Russian affairs who will be interacting with Russians in the coming years—businesspeople, government officials, consultants, scholars, scientists, and students as well as ordinary citizens.

The book is based on my more than twenty-five years of working with Russians—negotiating and facilitating people-to-people exchanges in culture, education, and science—both when Russia's relations with the United States were good and when they were not. Those years include service at the American Embassy in Moscow, numerous visits to the Soviet Union and Russia, and many years in Washington with the Department of State, United States Information Agency, Commission on Security and Cooperation in Europe (U.S. Congress), and National Endowment for Democracy.

When I first began to interact with Russians in the early 1960s, they had a well-earned reputation for being difficult. This was due, in part, to the Cold War mentality of the time on both sides. But another, more fundamental, factor was the inability of Americans and Russians to understand certain patterns of each other's behavior. This has led many to wonder why Russians are in some ways so similar to Americans and in other ways so different.

As U.S. journalists Peter Baker and Susan Glasser wrote after nearly four years (2001–2005) of reporting from Moscow to *The Washington Post:*

> For many Russians . . . politics remained little more than a corrupt form of warfare waged between equally unappealing clans. This was a view of the Putin-era battles shared even by many insiders who believed, as a disenchanted senior official put it to us, that the current shake-up was simply a fight for the financial spoils that came with control of the Kremlin. "The ideology is power and redistribution of property," the official said. "Power is a means of keeping property in their hands."[2] We heard this view whenever we asked regular Russians to explain the paradox of a country that embraced Putin but rejected many of his policies, where the public refused to participate in political life and claimed not to want democracy while cherishing rights like the freedom to travel and speak openly that had only been won with the Soviet collapse. These were contradictory times, as . . . when a new generation of cell-phone addicts could speak confidently about business school degrees one minute while bemoaning the collapse of the Soviet Union the next.[3]

There are, of course, risks in attempting to define national characteristics. A nation may be unfairly stereotyped, and there will always be exceptions to the rule. But who will not agree that Russians differ from Poles, Poles from Germans, and Germans from the French, although those nations have lived side by side in Europe from time immemorial? And Russians today in the Commonwealth of Independent States (CIS), as the successor to the Soviet Union is known, are recognizably different from Armenians, Georgians, and Moldovans, and even more different from Azeris, Kazakhs, and Uzbeks.[4]

The Russian character, formed over centuries by unique experiences and traditions, has made Russians distinct from other Europeans as well as from Americans. Many of those old characteristics continue today despite the revolutions of 1917, seventy years of communism, and its demise, and they will continue to influence whatever state and society evolve during the early years of the twenty-first century.

As French historian François Guizot wrote, looking back on his own country's revolutions:

> When nations have existed for a long and glorious time, they cannot break with their past, whatever they do; they are influenced by it at the very moment when they work to destroy it; in the midst of the most glaring transformations they remain fundamentally in character and destiny such as their history has formed them. Even the most daring and powerful revolutions cannot abolish national traditions of long duration. Therefore, it is most important, not only for the sake of intellectual curiosity but also for the good management of international relations, to know and to understand these traditions.[5]

Or, as A. P. Prokhorov, a modern-day Russian scholar has put it, "a nation, like an individual, cannot renounce its mentality, however much it may want to."[6]

ACKNOWLEDGMENTS

T HIS EDITION HAS BENEFITED from comments and suggestions on earlier editions received from many readers, both Russian and American. Particularly encouraging have been the favorable and complimentary letters received from Russians who do not understand how others perceive them. As one Russian writer, the author of many books about other cultures written for Russian readers, said, "Throughout my life as a writer, I have been taking literary 'snapshots' of other people, and now someone has taken a snapshot of me. It is very revealing."

I am also indebted to David Johnson for his *Johnson's Russia List,* a valuable resource for facts, figures, and commentary on contemporary Russia (see *www.cdi.org/russia/johnson*), and to the Kennan Institute of the Smithsonian Institution's Woodrow Wilson International Center for Scholars, where speakers, Russian as well as American, continue to enlighten audiences about the changes taking place these days in Russia.

Special thanks to Ben Eklof of Indiana University for his comments on Russian schools, and to Peter H. Solomon Jr. from the University of Toronto for his observations on Russian law.

In transliterating Russian names and words I have made some minor changes in the usual method in order to more closely approximate the Russian pronunciation. Where another spelling has become accepted usage in English, I have followed the more familiar form.

—Yale Richmond
Washington, D.C.

INTRODUCTION

M ANY AN AMERICAN has returned from a first visit to Russia exclaiming, "I don't understand why we have had such difficulties with the Russians. They're just like us." Subsequent visits—and a closer look—will reveal that Russians and Americans do indeed have differences. As a leading Soviet journalist, Vikenty Matveyev, once told me, "Americans will at first see the similarities between our two peoples, but they should also look for the differences."[7]

This book will seek to explain those differences and to help Americans understand why Russians behave like Russians. In the process, American readers may also learn why they behave like Americans.

The surface similarities are readily apparent. Russians feel a common identity with Americans as citizens of multiethnic, continental great powers. In history, both peoples have been expansionist. Americans moved west from the Atlantic coast across the Great Plains and Rocky Mountains to the Pacific shores. Russians expanded in all directions but mostly east across the Ural Mountains and the vast stretches of Siberia to the Pacific shores, and beyond to Alaska in 1741. Russians and Americans eventually met in 1812 in California, where so many new overtures seem to occur.

Both tamed a wilderness. Indeed, as Russian and American historians have noted, there is a frontier spirit shared by Siberia and the American West. The landowning gentry and the bonded serf of European Russia were not common to Siberia, which was settled by such diverse groups as Cossacks, political and religious dissidents, independent peasants, runaway serfs, and exiled convicts. Today's residents of the Siberian metropolis Novosibirsk liken it to Chicago, which they know by reputation as a hustling, bustling city serving a vast hinterland. And both Russians and Americans regard themselves as chosen nations with a messianic mission, destined to bring their own versions of enlightenment to less fortunate people.

America and Russia today are also nuclear powers with the capacity to destroy each other and the rest of the world as well. Likewise, both face the challenges of reducing their awesome arsenals of armaments and coping with the environmental consequences of their weapons industries.

Americans and Russians also think big. Both are energetic and inventive. Russians appreciate the casual, direct, and often blunt American way of speaking, which they liken to their own—without pretense and different from the West European manner, which they find too formal, indirect, and less sincere. And Russians, despite their traditional suspicion of foreigners, show heartfelt hospitality to visitors from abroad, a trait they share with Americans.

Differences between Russians and Americans are equally apparent. Authority in America has been diffused and flows upward from the people to a representative government. In Russia, authority has always been centralized and flows down. Pressure for change in the United States has come from below, and elected officials have either responded or eventually been replaced. Change in Russia has been imposed from above, and Russians have usually resisted because change there has been associated with hardship and misfortune.

In the United States, individuals are celebrated and their rights vis-à-vis government are protected in both law and practice. In Russia, from its earliest times, individual rights have been subordinated to the greater communal good. In the U.S., pluralism and tolerance for diverse views prevail. Such diversity appears chaotic to Russians, who value consensus and a single prevailing truth. The American economy is based in the private sector and a free market, and the role of government has been minor. Russian governments, whether tsarist, communist, or post-communist, have distrusted the free market and have played an active role in the economy. America's cultural roots are in Western Europe, while Russia's roots are in both Europe and Asia, and historians still debate which has played the greater role in shaping the Russian character.

Historical experience also separates Russians and Americans. For much of its history, Russia has been in a state of almost constant warfare with neighboring nations, and its people have often suffered extreme cruelties and violence in their own land. Since the Civil War, the United States has fought its wars mostly abroad, and its people have not known wartime hardship and devastation.

Whether similar or dissimilar, the two countries were thrust upon the world stage in the latter half of the twentieth century as nuclear superpowers and forced, rather reluctantly, to interact with each other. Only belatedly have they discovered the many common concerns they share, the most vital of which is the preservation of peace in the nuclear age.

These weighty concerns, however, have not always led to improved understanding. Contact between Russians and Americans in the past has been limited, separated as the two peoples have been by distance, ideology, and language. Today, however, they are interacting to an extent never before anticipated, and the need for improved understanding has become urgent not only for a few diplomats and businesspeople but for all Americans and Russians.

Examples of misunderstanding abound. After World War II the United States, unaware of the extent of the Soviet Union's devastation and losses, feared a Soviet assault on Western Europe. The Russians, in turn, regarded U.S. economic and military assistance to Western Europe as threats to their own security. Their field of vision narrowed by ideological blinders, they confidently awaited the collapse of capitalism and the triumph of what they called socialism. With the onset of the Cold War, paranoia grew on both sides.

The Cuban missile crisis of 1962, which brought the two superpowers to the brink of nuclear warfare, was the most frightful example of misjudgment. More recently, Mikhail Gorbachev's *glasnost* and *perestroika* were seen by some Americans as the start of a campaign to bring democracy to the Soviet Union. Other Americans, however, saw them as public relations gambits designed to deceive the West. Today, there are some who argue that Russia is no longer a great power and is irrelevant in international affairs. And how shall we view Vladimir Putin—as a genuine reformer or a reminder of Russia's authoritarian past, or both? Clearly, the gap in understanding still exists.

To help bridge that gap and enable readers to better understand the new Russia that is now evolving, this book will focus on those forces that have shaped Russian behavior in the past—geography, history, religion, culture, and governance—and how they differ from those that have formed American behavior.

The terms *Russian* and *Soviet* were often used interchangeably by both Russians and Americans. Even Soviet leaders at times incorrectly referred to the Soviet Union as Russia, even though Russia as a sovereign state ceased to exist in 1922 when it became part of the Union of Soviet Socialist Republics. And in December 1991, reflecting the discrediting of communism and the increased desire for sovereignty by the republics, the Soviet Union was transformed into a Commonwealth of Independent States, a loose political alliance whose permanence may also be questioned.

Our subject here will be the Russians rather than all of the more than one hundred nationalities that comprised the Soviet people. While Russians numbered little more than half the population of the former Soviet Union, the political and economic leadership was almost entirely Russian, as were the top echelons of the Communist Party, the armed forces, and the KGB. Russian, moreover, was the predominant language and culture.

Whether Russian or Soviet, many changes have been occurring in that distant land, which Winston Churchill in 1939 described as "a riddle, wrapped in a mystery, inside an enigma." Today we know much more about that riddle, but each day's news records events that no one, including Russians, could have foreseen only a few years ago. Russia's mystery has moderated but the enigma remains.

The nature of the recent changes can legitimately be questioned—are they real, and how long will they last? Is Russia heading toward democracy or autocracy, and what role will Putin or Medvedev play? But whatever the results of Russia's most recent effort to modernize, change there will continue to be shaped by the Russian character, and that character, formed over a millennium, has changed slowly.

Russia was a communist country for seventy years but has been Russian Orthodox for a thousand, and Russians have lived even longer with their harsh climate, vast expanse of forest and steppe, and geographic and cultural isolation. To understand the Russians, one must know whence they come.

ONE

Welcome to Moscow

M Y PLANE TO MOSCOW was late, arriving in the dark at
Sheremetyevo Airport on a winter evening many years ago
after a long flight from New York. It was not a warm welcome. The wind was
bitterly cold as passengers deplaned and piled aboard a bus with frosted-over
windows for the short ride to the terminal. I had been traveling since the
previous evening and was tired.

Inside the terminal the wait at immigration was long and tedious as
young, grim-faced border guards took their time checking passports and
visas. The customs clearance was equally long and thorough, but at last I was
cleared and once more admitted to Russia.

Russian airport terminals are crowded, noisy, and chaotic as passengers
mill about seeking friends and greeters. As elsewhere in the East, airport
arrivals and departures bring out throngs of relatives and well-wishers, but
not for me. Alone with my luggage, I struggled to the head of the taxi line.

After a thirty-minute drive to the city and a hassle with the taxi driver—
Russia's most zealous capitalists—who wanted to be paid in dollars, I arrived
at the Ukraina. Unlike Moscow's newer hotels, the old Ukraina was built in
the "wedding cake" style of the Stalin era and had a musty decor that
reminded a visitor of old Russia. I first stayed at the hotel in 1963 and over
the years had become accustomed to its shabby and faded inelegance.

There was no line at the registration desk, just the usual crowd pushing, shoving, and trying to get the attention of the lone clerk. After a

fifteen-minute wait, I finally registered, gave my bags to a porter, showed my hotel identification card to the ever-present guard who admitted me to the inner lobby, and was on my way to an upper floor. One final hassle occurred before I was settled in my room—the porter demanded to be tipped in dollars or with a pack of Marlboros, the preferred brand in Russia.

It was then that hunger hit. I had not eaten since a light lunch on my flight and was looking forward to a snack at the hotel *bufet,* a sort of Russian snack bar. But to eat at the bufet I first had to change my dollars into rubles, since Soviet currency in those years could not legally be brought into the Soviet Union.

Making my way down the long dim hall, I approached the *dyezhurnaya* (person on duty) for my floor. A feature of many Russian hotels, they are the women who keep the keys, control access to rooms, and provide hot water for tea or instant coffee. Inquiring about the location of the currency exchange office, I was told that it had closed for the day.

"*Shto delat?*" (What to do?), I asked, a common Russian expression.

Shrugging her shoulders, the old woman looked me over indifferently. Here was the making of a classic confrontation between a Western visitor and the Soviet system, which was not designed to serve individuals with special requests. Had I been a member of a tour group, there would have been a guide to tend to my needs, and dinner would have been planned for the group at the hotel restaurant, paid in advance, and there would have been no need to change money. But here I was, a lone traveler who had to get something to eat before falling into bed to catch up with the eight-hour time change from New York.

From past experience in Russia I knew not to retreat, so I stood my ground, changed the subject, and began to converse with the woman. We talked about my long trip from the States, the purpose of my visit, the Moscow weather, where I had learned to speak Russian, her children and mine, and how nice it was for me to be back in Russia again. After a while, I returned to the subject of my hunger and asked if she had any suggestions as to what I might do before the snack bar closed for the night.

"I'll lend you some rubles," she replied, reaching for her *sumka* (satchel) under the desk, "and you can pay me back tomorrow."

My approach had worked. A kind Russian grandmother had taken pity on a hungry American and lent him a few of her own rubles so he could get some *khleb, sir, i chai* (bread, cheese, and tea) before retiring for the night. Welcome to Moscow!

The lesson of that story—and this book—is simple. Russia can be a cold and impersonal place, where a visitor's requests are all too often met with an automatic *nyet*. But Russians respond to a human approach, and they can be warm and helpful once a good interpersonal relationship has been established. When that point is reached, their word is good, *nyet* becomes *da,* and deals can be done. That is the key to understanding the Russians.

TWO

Geography and Culture

All civilizations are to some extent the product of geographical factors, but history provides no clearer example of the profound influence of geography upon a culture than in the historical development of the Russian people.

—George Vernadsky, *A History of Russia*

THE ORIGINS OF RUSSIA

One Rus has its roots in a universal, or at least European, culture. In this Rus the ideas of goodness, honor and freedom are understood as in the West. But there is another Rus: the Rus of the dark forests, the Rus of the Taiga, the animal Russia, the fanatic Russia, the Mongol-Tatar Russia. This last Russia made despotism and fanaticism its ideal. . . . Kievan Rus was a part of Europe, Moscow remained the negation of Europe.

—Leo Tolstoy

Mikhail Gorbachev, in 1989, endorsed the concept of a "common European home" with Russia as a tenant.[8] In geographic terms, the common European home makes sense. Europe does extend from the Atlantic Ocean to the Ural Mountains, and Russia—at least a part of it—is indeed in Europe. But through much of its history, Russia has been isolated from or has rejected Europe and its Western ways. Gorbachev's common European home, with

5

Russia occupying the back porch and the United States and Canada the front porch, was a new concept in geopolitical real estate.

The great rivers of Russia flow north and south, and along those rivers came Russia's early contacts with the outside world. From the northern rivers in the ninth century came Viking raiders and traders from Scandinavia who became the rulers of Rus, the city-principality of Kiev and the forerunner of the Russian state. From the southern rivers came contacts with Byzantium, the Eastern half of the Christian Roman Empire, and its resplendent capital, the Greek city of Constantinople (today's Istanbul), whence came Russia's religion, law, and art.

Kievan Rus converted to Orthodox Christianity in 988, and Constantinople became its link to the Mediterranean and the West for commerce as well as culture. But scarcely a century later that linkage was threatened by repeated onslaughts of mounted marauders from Asia moving westward over the great Eurasian steppe. When those invaders reached the Kievan Rus state and threatened its capital, the Rus began to migrate north, seeking protection in remote forests inhabited at that time by Finnish tribes. Power gradually shifted from Kievan Rus to Russian Muscovy.

The Mongols (called *Tatars* in early Russian sources) invaded Russia in the mid-thirteenth century.[9] Unstoppable, they took Moscow in 1234 and Kiev in 1240, and they made Russian princes their vassals for the next two hundred years. While the Mongol-Tatar conquest did not make Asians of the Russians, it did delay their becoming Europeans. It also produced today's Russians—a mixture of Slavic, Finnish, and Tatar blood.

When Moscow liberated itself from the Tatar yoke in 1480, the modern Russian state was born. Distant from Europe, the new state was cut off from Constantinople, which, in 1453, had fallen to the Muslim Ottoman Turks. The Russian Orthodox Church, isolated from the rest of Christianity, developed independently as a national church.

Moscow, moreover, saw itself as the third and last Rome, successor to Rome and Constantinople, the two capitals of the Roman Empire, which in turn had fallen to barbarians and infidels. Russia was regarded by its religious and lay leaders as a holy land with an imperial mission—a new center of Christianity destined to unite the peoples of East and West. It was at that time that Russian rulers began to use the title *tsar,* derived from the Latin *Caesar.*

Russia's historic distrust of the West has its roots in that religious schism and its aftermath. Remote from the West, Russia experienced none of the major developments that shaped modern Europe—the Renaissance with its

6

revival of classical influence and flowering of the arts, the Reformation with its pluralism of religious and secular thought, the rise of big cities, the development of modern agriculture and commerce, the scientific revolution, economic liberalism and recognition of individual rights, the beginnings of political liberty, and the growth of a strong middle class. In the West the middle class was in the forefront of reform. Russia's failure to develop a strong middle class delayed reform.

Cut off from the West, Russia remained a vast, backward, largely agricultural empire, regimented and ruled by an autocratic dynasty with a holy mission to defend its faith against the barbarians of the East and the heresies and pluralism of the West.

The pluralism of the West, moreover, was seen by Russia as chaotic, a cacophony of voices without harmony, a disunity of thought and purpose. To that West, nevertheless, Russia would come during its periodic attempts to modernize, seeking science, technology, and administrative know-how, but rejecting at the same time the Western ways that came with the modernization it so sorely needed.

To remote Russia many things Western have come late—manufacturing, higher education, science and technology, the management sciences, and computers, as well as blue jeans and rock music. Other things Western have not yet arrived—good government, transparency, and efficiency. Those come from a West that Russia has openly disdained but secretly envied, and from which it is today again trying to learn.

THE COLD NORTH

The aim of civilization in the North is serious. There, society is the fruit, not of human pleasures, not of interests and passions easily satisfied, but of a will ever persisting and ever thwarted which urges the people to incomprehensible efforts. There, if individuals unite together, it is to struggle with a rebellious nature, which unwillingly responds to the demands made upon her.

—Marquis de Custine, *Empire of the Czar*

Mention the Russian winter and most people will think of deep snow piled to the rooftops. Actually, the snow is not that deep in Russia, and winter there is known more for its frigid temperatures, which Russians find invigorating. They break out their winter clothing, fur hats, cross-country skis, and their *valenki,* the felt boots that have kept Russian feet warm through the centuries and that have now become very stylish in the West. Russians seem to enjoy their cold winters, but those winter temperatures can become unbearable when the wind blows across the open land and the windchill factor plummets.

Russia is a northern country. Moscow lies on the same latitude as the lower Hudson Bay, and Russia's northernmost port, Murmansk, is further north than Nome, Alaska. Its most southern port, Novorossisk, on the Black Sea, is on the same latitude as Minneapolis.

Nature has not been kind to Russia. Much of European Russia and Siberia is very cold most of the year, similar to Canada and the U.S. northern plains states. Autumn is brief, followed by a long and cold winter. Summers are short and hot. In old Russia, where the economy was mostly agricultural, peasants could do little during the winter months, and they more or less hibernated, holed up in their huts, seeking to survive while awaiting spring and the sowing season.

When spring did arrive, there was much to be done in a short span of time. In Russia's northern lands there is less than five months from spring, when the ground can be tilled and seeded, until fall, when crops must be harvested before the first frost. During those precious few months, Russians over the centuries have worked almost around the clock to produce the food needed to get them through the following winter.

According to one popular theory, that explains why Russians often appear inactive for long periods of time and then show intense bursts of energy. The stagnation of the Brezhnev era, for example, can be seen as a long winter of hibernation, and the perestroika of the Gorbachev years as a short spring and summer of frenzied effort.

The harsh climate also explains the strength of Russians, their ability to endure extreme hardship, and their bleak outlook on life, as well as their patience and submission. Climate has also made them cautious. In Russia's farmlands weather is often unpredictable, and crop failure is an ever-present possibility. In an agricultural society where survival depends on the weather, it is imprudent to take chances. And as in all traditional societies, the test of time is preferred to the risks of the new and untried.

Does climate still make a difference in the early years of the twenty-first century? Over millennia, people everywhere have adapted to their environment, and today some have even tamed it. Americans, with central heating, air conditioning, and other modern conveniences, have literally insulated themselves from weather's extremes. American culture and character today are not much different in Minnesota than in states with milder climes.

Russians, however, have been living in their cold north for millennia, and, for much of that time, as serfs and peasants in a primitive agricultural society. Until recently, most Russians have lived much as their ancestors have before them—in small villages, distant and isolated, their freedom of movement restricted, and without the comforts and labor-saving tools provided by modern society. The cold north is very much in their bones and psyches.

A Russian winter has to be lived through to be really appreciated. Winter starts in October and continues through March, with November to January the darkest months. St. Petersburg, at the winter solstice, has only five and one-half hours of daylight, and on days with overcast skies and smog there is often no sun to be seen. In the Russian far north during the dead of winter, the sun never rises at all.[10]

During the winter months, many Russians suffer from Seasonal Affective Disorder (SAD), as the ailment is known in the West. Anger, hostility, fatigue, and depression increase, as well as the demand for psychiatric services. Vodka consumption rises, alcoholic treatment centers overflow, and suicides rise. Hundreds of homeless people die of hypothermia. Political discontent reaches its peak.

DISTANCE AND ISOLATION

Forced to withdraw into the northeastern corner of Europe and to use all their strength there in the difficult labor of national unification, the Russian people found themselves, from the thirteenth century on, physically separated from the rest of the Christian world.

—S. M. Solovyov, *Peter's Reforms*

Most countries have only one time zone. The United States has six, and Americans in the East who watch a football game in California know that there is a three-hour time difference. Russia, however, has eleven time zones and is almost twice as large as the United States, stretching six thousand miles from west to east. A trip from Moscow to Vladivostok on the Pacific via the famous Trans-Siberian Railway covers more than one-third the globe's circumference and takes seven days.

That vast landmass—one-eighth of the earth's land surface—has only limited access to the sea. Deep in its Eurasian remoteness, Russia has been distant from Europe, the Mediterranean, the Middle East, China, and other great centers of civilization. Moscow is 1,500 miles from Paris, and before the age of the railroad, such an arduous and dangerous journey could take several months.

The two momentous events mentioned earlier—the Mongol-Tatar invasions of the thirteenth century, which cut Russia off from Europe for almost 250 years, and the fall of Constantinople, the center of Eastern Christianity, to the Turks in 1453—caused Russia's commercial, cultural, and religious isolation, and delayed its development for centuries, a handicap that it has never fully overcome.

Distance and isolation also deterred development of a mercantile tradition. Self-sufficient in agriculture and natural resources, and with no great need to trade with other countries, Russia became inwardly oriented. Contacts with the outside world were through neighboring states, and when conflicts arose with those states, they were often resolved by military force, resulting in Russia's annexation of more and more new lands.

Geography also made Russia vulnerable to wars—literally hundreds of them—along her lengthy borders, which have no natural defenses. To the east, the great Eurasian steppe served as a highway for waves of invaders from Asia who, in ancient times, repeatedly swept into Russia. From the west, Russia has been invaded by Teutonic Knights, Lithuanians, Poles, Swedes, the French, and Germans. And to the south, Russia has had continuous wars over the centuries with Turkic tribes.

As a result of that constant border warfare, Russia became the largest state—actually an empire—on earth. Its expansion, moreover, resulted in even longer undefined borders as well as heightened suspicion of neighboring nations.

With such a vast territory to govern, Russia evolved into a state ruled from its center and organized along paramilitary lines. Service to the state was a duty for both nobles and peasants. Surrounded by hostile powers, Russia became dependent on the use of force in its relations with neighboring states and obsessed with security, traits that still survive. Although the Mongols invaded Russia some seven hundred years ago, the memory of their rule is one reason for Russia's deep-rooted suspicion of China today. But that fear is perhaps understandable, considering the economically expanding China with more than one billion of its people on one side of an indefensible and oft-contested border, and a vast and relatively empty resource-rich Siberia on the other side. Visitors to Russia should avoid making comparisons with China, which can provoke visceral reactions among Russians.

How has a state ringed by so many adversaries been able continually to extend its territorial reach? As Russians see it, they have been victims of foreign aggression, and Russia's expansion is the result of victories over foreign invaders. As others see it, Russia has taken advantage of weakness or instability in neighboring states to annex territories along her periphery.

One sharp critic of Russian territorial aggrandizement in the mid-nineteenth century was a London-based correspondent of *The New York Tribune* named Karl Marx. In 1852, in his coverage of events leading to the Crimean War, Marx wrote:

> Russia's acquisitions from Sweden are greater than what remains of that kingdom; from Poland, nearly equal to the Austrian empire; from Turkey in Europe, greater than Prussia (exclusive of the Rhenish provinces); from Turkey in Asia, as large as the whole dominion of Germany proper; from Persia, equal to England; from Tartary, to an extent as large as European Turkey, Greece, Italy, and Spain, taken together. The total acquisitions of Russia during the last sixty years are equal in extent and importance to the whole Empire she had in Europe before that time.[11]

Along with her territorial expansion, Russia sought protection from foreign influence. Periodic attempts to introduce European technology and Western ways met with the sullen resistance of most of the Russian people. Suspicion and mistrust of foreigners—and the West in particular—have been a recurring theme in both Russian and Soviet history, and the Iron Curtain of the Soviet era was its most recent manifestation. New ideas have come late to Russia, when they have come at all.

The United States has also been a continental power and expansionist, but with a maritime and commercial tradition. The Atlantic and Pacific oceans served as natural defenses, providing protection from foreign aggression and ensuring the stability necessary for economic development at home and trade abroad. The American fixation with freedom of the seas can be compared with Russia's obsession with security along her borders. The objective of both countries has been to ensure stability and well-being at home.

The United States' commercial experience and Russia's lack of a mercantile tradition have given the two countries different world outlooks. As Harvard's Richard Pipes points out, "Commerce is . . . by its very nature conducive to compromise. Nations raised on it instinctively seek a common ground for agreement, that exact point at which the other side might be prepared to make a deal."[12] Compromise is native to America but alien to Russia.

The oceans, moreover, have been bridges for the United States, providing easy access to other countries and cultures. New ideas have usually been welcomed, or at least not opposed, and the oceans served as highways for waves of immigrants who came in peace and with hope, turning their backs on the rigid class divisions of the Old World to seek a better life in the New. They brought vitality and talent to a constantly changing and dynamic society.

The New World is indeed new, only some 400 years old, compared to Russia's more than 1,000. Russians, moreover, have been living in their native environment from time immemorial, and change has come slowly. The new has been welcomed in America; the old has been revered in Russia.

COMMUNALISM

[For Russians] the striving for corporate forms of activity has always prevailed over individualism.

—Vladimir Putin, *First Person*

Sobornost (communal spirit, togetherness) distinguishes Russians from Westerners, for whom individualism and competitiveness are more common characteristics. As Nicolas Zernov, the late Russian Orthodox theologian, explained, in Russia there is the desire ". . . to find the balance between the conflicting outlooks of Europe and Asia, between Western claims to personal freedom and Oriental insistence on the integration of the individual into the community."[13]

Russia, writes Nina Khrushcheva, a great-granddaughter of Nikita Khrushchev,

> had always valued the communal way of life over the merely individual. Community was seen so near to the ideal of brotherly love, which forms the essence of Christianity and thus represents the higher mission of the people. In this "higher mission" a commune—a triumph of human spirit— was understood as opposing law, formal organizations, and personal interests.[14]

Russian communalism was not an invention of communists, although its traditions were exploited under the Soviets. The affinity for the group has deep roots in Russian culture, and its origins can be traced to the vastness of the great Russian plain.

In prehistoric times Russians banded together to fell the forest, till the soil, harvest the crops, and protect themselves from invaders and marauders. Tools and weapons were primitive and life was harsh, but those handicaps could be overcome and survival ensured—although just barely—by the collective effort of living and working together.

The *zadruga,* a clan or greater family commune, served as the nucleus of a tribal society. In time, it evolved into a larger unit, the *mir,* an agricultural village commune (also known as *obshchina*) based on territory and mutual interests. Member families lived in small hamlets, in huts side by side. The surrounding land was held in common by the mir and was unfenced. Each family, however, had its own hut, maintained a small plot of land for a family garden, and took its meals at home.[15]

Land utilization was the mir's primary purpose and the basis for its survival. The mir determined how much of the common land each family would work, depending on its size and needs. It decided which crops would be grown and when they would be planted and harvested. It collected taxes and settled local disputes. The mir's authority, moreover, extended beyond land matters: It also disciplined members, intervened in family disputes, settled issues that affected the community as a whole, and otherwise regulated the affairs of its self-contained and isolated agricultural world.

The word *mir,* in fact, has three meanings in Russian—village commune, world, and peace—and for its members it symbolized all three. That little world of the Russian peasant—the bulk of the populace—was a world apart from, and at least a century behind, the lifestyles of landowners and city dwellers.

Decisions of the mir were made in a village assembly of heads of households. All members could speak and discussions were lively, but no vote was taken. The objective was to determine the collective will, and after an issue had been thoroughly discussed and opposition to it had ceased, a consensus evolved that became binding on all households. Richard Stites describes the mir meetings as marked by "seemingly immense disorder and chaos, interruptions, and shouting; in fact it achieved business-like results."[16]

When peasants moved to cities as workers and craftsmen, they brought with them their communal way of life and formed workers' cooperatives called *artels.* Modeled on the mir, artel members hired themselves out for jobs as a group and shared the payments for their work. Some artels rented communal apartments where they would share the rent, buy the food, dine together, and even attend leisure events as a group. Hundreds of thousands of workers lived in this way in the generation or so before the Bolshevik Revolution.[17] In the city, as in the village, security and survival were ensured by a collective effort.

That communal way of life persisted well into the twentieth century, lasting longer in Russia than elsewhere in Europe. Tsarist Russia encouraged the mir because it served as a form of state control over the peasants and facilitated tax collection and military conscription. Because the mir affected so many people, and for such a long time, it played a major role in forming the Russian character. In the late 1950s, for example, when Soviet students began to come to the United States and were assigned in groups to American universities, they would often pool their stipends, live off a small part of their pooled funds, and save as much as they could for later purchases.[18]

As Lev Tikhomirov—appropriately, with a mir in the middle of his name—wrote in 1888, "The Great Russian cannot imagine a life outside his society, outside the mir. . . . The Great Russian says: 'The mir is a fine fellow, I will not desert the mir. Even death is beautiful in common.' "[19]

Serfdom (personal bondage) was imposed on most Russian peasants in the late sixteenth century and lasted for three hundred years before being abolished in 1861 (the Emancipation Proclamation ended slavery in the United States in 1863). The emancipation of serfs was accompanied by a land redistribution that enabled serfs, in principle, to purchase land outside the commune. However, land distributed under the reform was actually given to the mir, which held it in common until its members could make redemption payments.

That freed the serfs but preserved the mir, and peasants once more found themselves bound to the land they worked, since most of them were financially unable to leave the commune. The reform thus continued the mir's power over peasants and their submission to a higher authority that regulated the social order.

Service to the state also continued. The emancipation was accompanied by a reduction in the length of obligatory military service for former serfs and the lower class of townspeople. After 1861, the length of duty for those selected was reduced from twenty-five to sixteen years! A later reform, in 1874, made military service compulsory for all able-bodied males over age twenty; the tour of active duty was further reduced to six years but was followed by nine years in the reserve and five more in the *militsia* (police).

The mir endured in various forms until the early 1930s, when it was replaced by yet another form of communal life, the Soviet collective farm.

A modern-day effort by the state to tie peasants to the land, the brutally enforced collectivization was strongly opposed by the peasants, especially in Ukraine. The objective was to ensure an adequate supply of food for the cities, which were to grow under the industrialization of the Five-Year Plans. The immediate result, however, was famine and the death of millions in the countryside.

The contrast between Russian communalism and American individualism can best be seen in the differences between Russian peasants and American farmers. America's agricultural settlers were independent farmers and ranchers who owned their own land and lived on it, self-sufficient and distant from their neighbors. In contrast to peasants of the mir, American farmers lived behind fences that marked the limits of their property. The Americans, moreover, were entrepreneurs in the sense that they managed their holdings individually, taking economic risks and regulating their own affairs, independent of the state.

The United States also has had its communes—and still has some today—an indication of some innate human urge to band and bond together. These communes, however, have existed on the fringes of society rather than at its center. In the U.S., the commune is considered alien (unless Native Americans, who also lived a communal lifestyle, are considered). To Russians, the commune is native.

Individualism is esteemed in the West, but in Russian the word has a pejorative meaning. Steeped in the heritage of the mir, Russians think of themselves as members of a community rather than as individuals. Communal spirit helps to explain many of their characteristics—behavior in crowds, for example. Physical contact with complete strangers—anathema to Americans and West Europeans—does not bother Russians. In crowds, they touch, push, shove, and even use elbows without hard feelings—except in the ribs of those who are competing with them to obtain access to something. Visitors to Russia should not take such pokes personally. Politeness takes different forms in different societies, and behavior in crowds can vary.

A crowd of passengers attempting to board a ship in Odessa in the early 1960s caught the attention of British traveler Laurens van der Post. A ship's officer stood on the quay collecting tickets at the gangway. The crowd pushed and jostled but never lost its temper. Although it shouted at the officer and elbowed him out of the way, he did not appear irritated, nor did he attempt to call them to order. A Russian friend related to van der Post how a group of French tourists, caught earlier in the same situation and annoyed by the crowd's persistent jostling, had lost their tempers and lashed out angrily at everyone near them. "The Russians were horrified at such lack of traveling manners," wrote van der Post, "presumably because it was personal retaliation and not the collective, impersonal pressure they were all applying to get through a bottleneck."[20] Foreign visitors who are averse to close contact should avoid the Moscow Metro (subway) during rush hours, when trains run every 90 seconds, although they are still crowded the rest of the day. Nevertheless, it's an inexpensive way to get around the city and avoid the horrendous street traffic, but watch your wallet! Taxis may seem more convenient, but they are expensive and the price should be negotiated before you get in. And do not enter if there is another passenger in the car. Safety first!

Accustomed to close physical contact, Russian men, as well as women, touch when talking. Women dance with other women if there are not enough men to go around or if not asked by a man for a dance. Russian men embrace and kiss each other, on the lips as well as cheeks, as I learned once when I had a male kiss planted on my lips, much to my surprise, at the end of a long and festive evening. Americans are advised, however, not to initiate such spontaneous displays of affection, as President Jimmy Carter learned when he kissed Leonid Brezhnev (on the cheek) at their Vienna summit meeting, much to Brezhnev's surprise and embarrassment.

Recreational activities are often arranged in groups, as in the artel. After working together all day, factory and office employees will spend evenings in group excursions to theaters and other cultural events organized by their shop stewards.

Russians seem compelled to intrude into the private affairs of others. Older Russians admonish young men and women—complete strangers—for perceived wrongdoings, using the patronizing term of address *molodoy chelovek* (young man) or *dyevushka* (girl). On the streets, older women volunteer advice to young mothers on the care of their children. American parents in Moscow have been accosted by Russian women and accused of not dressing their children properly for the severe winter. One American, whose child was clad in well-insulated outerwear, would respond by unzipping her child's jacket and inviting the Russian women to feel how warm her child's body actually was. In a collective society, everybody's business is also everyone else's. (One intrusion that is appreciated, and expected, is to inform others when they show the telltale white skin blotches that indicate the onset of frostbite.)

Russians do not hesitate to visit a friend's home without advance notice, even dropping in unexpectedly late at night as long as a light can be seen in a window. They routinely offer overnight accommodations to friends who are visiting their cities, a gesture based not only on their tradition of hospitality to travelers but also on the shortage of affordable hotel accommodations. Americans who are accepted as friends by Russians will find that they too may receive unexpected visits and requests for lodging from their new friends.

NATIONALITY

Throughout Russian history one dominating theme has been the frontier; the theme of the struggle of the mastering of the resources of an untamed country, expanded into a continent by the ever-shifting movement of the Russian people and their conquest of and intermingling with other peoples.

—B. H. Sumner, *A Short History of Russia*

No greater mistake can be made by a visitor to Russia than to assume that every Russian-speaking person encountered will be an ethnic Russian. The Russian Federation, the name of the new Russia, is a multinational state comprising people of many different nations whom, as British historian B. H. Sumner reminded us, the Russians conquered and intermingled with in their expansion throughout history.

The difference is nationality—the "nation" or ethnic group that an individual belongs to, which number some 176 in today's Russia. They include such people as Bashkirs, Buryats, Chechens, Chuvash, Ingush, Kalmyks, Komis, Mordvinians, Ossetians, Tatars, Yakuts, and many others, all with their own cultures and languages. According to the CIA's *World Factbook*, as many as 10 to 15 percent of the Russian population are practicing Muslims.[21] Moreover, their birth rate is much higher than that of ethnic Russians, which concerns Russians as their own birth rate declines. Also of concern to Russians is the ethnic consciousness among some of the minorities and their desire for autonomy or self-rule.

Russia's territorial expansion began in the sixteenth century, and over the next three hundred years it annexed along its periphery—north, south, east, and west—lands with non-Russian peoples. How to deal with those nationalities in a vast empire ruled from its Russian center has been a challenge to Russian tsars, Soviet commissars, and now the elected leaders of the new Russia.

Throughout much of modern history, the Russians were a bare majority in their own country. That changed with the breakup of the Soviet Union, and today ethnic Russians number some 80 percent of the 141 million people of the Russian Federation.[22]

Despite the loss of many of its peripheral lands, Russia today is still a vast state, extending from St. Petersburg (formerly Leningrad) to the Sea of Japan, comprising three-fourths of the territory of the former Soviet Union, with little more than half its population but with most of its natural resources—oil, gas, coal, gold, diamonds, and timber, among others.

Of the Russian Federation's more than 80 administrative units, 31 are so-called autonomous entities where most of the non-Russians live—in 16 autonomous republics, 5 autonomous regions, and 10 autonomous districts. Together, these entities comprise about half the area of the Russian Federation and contain most of its natural and mineral resources. In these "autonomies," Russian is the lingua franca, intermarriage with Russians is common, and the population has been heavily "Russified." In 26 of the 31 autonomies, Russians are in the majority.

In some autonomies, however, ethnic consciousness is high, as in Chechnya, a non-Slavic, largely Muslim republic in the Caucasus Mountains. Chechnya is the size of Connecticut and has a population of 1.2 million, of whom one million are Chechens. Russia brought Chechnya under its control and annexed it in 1864, after a bitter guerrilla war that lasted several decades. But nationalism remained high, and in 1944, during World War II, Joseph Stalin exiled the entire Chechen population to Soviet Central Asia, from which the survivors were allowed to return only some ten years later. In 1991, Chechnya declared its independence from the Russian Federation, and a civil war followed in which more than 100,000 Chechens and Russians were killed before a truce was signed in 1996. Despite several cease fires, fighting resumed in 1999 and continued as Russia once more sought to impose a military solution on a political problem. As of this writing, Chechnya has been "pacified," although the potential for further violence continues.

The movement for autonomy or self-rule is also strong in areas with Russian majorities where local leaders seek increased independence and financial gain by loosening political and economic ties with the Moscow central government. Ethnic and local consciousness is on the rise in Russia, and people who interact with Russians and other ethnic groups should appreciate its significance.

Prior to its breakup in 1991, the Soviet Union had a population of 290 million and was the world's third most populous country, after China and India. Predominant were the three Slavic nations that speak related languages and share a common Christian heritage—Russians, with a little more than

50 percent of the Soviet population; Ukrainians, 18 percent; and Belarusians, 3.6 percent. Other major Soviet nationalities with a Christian heritage were Georgians and Armenians, 3 percent; Lithuanians, Latvians, and Estonians, 3 percent; and Moldovans, 1 percent.

Nations with an Islamic or Turkic heritage were another 20 percent of the Soviet population, with Azeri, Kazakh, Kyrgyz, Tajik, Tatar, Turkmen, and Uzbek the major nationalities. And in the far north lived Arctic peoples with cultures similar to those of their North American cousins.

Nationality and religion are interrelated. Russians and Belarusians are Russian Orthodox. Ukrainians may be Ukrainian Autocephalous Orthodox, Russian Orthodox, or, in western Ukraine, which for centuries was a part of Poland, Ukrainian Catholic (Uniate), a church that uses the Eastern rite but is in union with the Roman Catholic Church in recognizing the authority of the Pope. Armenians and Georgians, who have their own churches, have been Christian since A.D. 301 and A.D. 318 respectively. Lithuanians are Roman Catholic by virtue of having been part of the Polish-Lithuanian Commonwealth for four centuries. Latvians and Estonians are Lutheran, a heritage of their German colonization and Swedish rule. Moldovans, like their fellow Romanians, are Orthodox.

Responding to the challenge of Zionism, the Soviet Union in 1928 established a Jewish Autonomous Region around Birobidzhan on the China border. Birobidzhan, however, has never attracted many Jews, and today they number only 3 percent of the local population.

Belarus and western Ukraine, as noted earlier, were under Polish rule from the fourteenth to the eighteenth centuries, and western portions of those lands were again a part of Poland between the two world wars. As a result, many Ukrainians and Belarusians appear more Western than do Russians. Ukraine, moreover, is located in a southern, more temperate zone and was known as the breadbasket of Russia and Europe. As "southerners," Ukrainians tend to be more outgoing and optimistic than their northern cousins.

The three Baltic republics were recognized as independent by Moscow in September 1991. All the other Soviet republics, except Ukraine, followed their lead in December, but, as sovereign states, the Baltics chose not to join the Commonwealth of Independent States (CIS), which replaced the Soviet Union. And on 14 August 2008 the Georgian parliament, in response to the Soviet invasion of Georgia, voted unanimously to withdraw from the CIS, a decision that requires 12 months to implement. To further complicate this ethnic mosaic, some twenty million Russians, known as the "Near Abroad," live outside the Russian Federation in the other former Soviet republics. There, they are a potential source of conflict with local governments, and the Russian Federation feels responsible for their welfare. In many parts of the Russian Federation there are also Germans, Poles, Jews, and other nationalities that do not have their own designated territories. Although interest in local languages has increased in recent years, Russian is still the lingua franca of the CIS, the language Uzbeks use to talk with Russians, and Armenians to Azeris (when they are talking to each other).

Americans also live in a multinational or multicultural state that has one dominant language and culture, "Anglo." Americans may therefore find it difficult to comprehend the complexity of Russian nationality problems and to appreciate their political importance.

The difference lies in two almost contradictory aspects of American culture. One is America's role as a melting pot during its first 175 years of nationhood, absorbing waves of immigrants from many parts of Europe, who in time assimilated into the dominant American culture. Within a few generations the old-world languages of the immigrants were largely lost, and cultural ties to the old country became mostly a matter of sentiment. In recent years, an influx of Hispanics and Asians has created a large body of Americans who take pride in their cultural and linguistic diversity; Americans, however, recognize that theirs is a pluralistic society composed of different backgrounds and races, and they pride themselves on their ability to create unity in diversity.

In Russia, ethnic diversity is a completely different phenomenon, based on centuries of residence by various nationalities in their historic regions of origin and on the determination of many of them to preserve their distinct languages and cultures.

In Western and Central Europe, nationality as a political issue was largely resolved during the late nineteenth and early twentieth centuries. To be sure, the formation of new nation-states and the redrawing of national borders, particularly after World War I, did not impose perfect solutions. Nationality conflicts continue today in Belgium, Bulgaria, Romania, Slovakia, Spain, and the former Yugoslavia. But, with the exception of Yugoslavia, nationality differences have not threatened the existence of those states.

In the East, however, nationalism and ethnicity reemerged in the 1990s to threaten the stability of several states. Centuries-old ethnic and national rivalries and passions have resurfaced and resulted in violence between non-

Russian nationalities—Armenians and Azeris, Uzbeks and Mshkets, Georgians and Abkhazians, and Chechens and Ingush. Attempts by Moscow at Russification are resisted today by some as strongly as they were under the tsars and the Soviets.

In response to those ethnic stirrings, there has been a resurgence of Russian nationalism and a renewed interest in Russian Orthodoxy. Most Russians regret the breakup of the Soviet Union, and there is considerable Russian sentiment for a union of Russia with Belarus and Ukraine in a greater Slav state, including perhaps the northern half of Kazakhstan, where some five million Russians live and where the population is largely Russian.

Rising Russian nationalism, unfortunately, has been accompanied by emerging ethnic and racial violence. Newly found freedoms have enabled Russians to express previously repressed prejudices. People from the Caucasus and Central Asia, as well as others who do not appear to be Russian, are often victims of abuse, harassment, and violence. The main victims have been Azeris, Chechens, Georgians, and Roma (Gypsies). Blacks may also be victims of verbal abuse and assaults on the streets.

Anti-Semitism, long latent in Russia (and at times not so latent), has also resurfaced. Jews have been subjected to harassment and violence, particularly in provinces where local leaders beyond Moscow's control resort to anti-Semitism for political purposes. Nevertheless, the mass exodus to Israel and other countries has ended, and there has been a renaissance of Jewish life for Russia's estimated 600,000 to one million Jews. The number of Jewish communities is believed to be about one hundred, and they are found in all regions of the country. People of Jewish descent are prominent in science, medicine, literature, and the arts, as well as in politics and public life. Anti-Semitism, once state policy under the Soviets, has been disavowed by the Russian government.

The main perpetrators of ethnic violence are skinheads, young men in their late teens who shave their heads and dress in combat gear. Some are affiliated with groups of *futbol* (soccer) fans; others are linked to a neo-Nazi movement. All share a hatred of "foreigners," among whom they include Jews and others whose families have lived in Russia for centuries.

Russians and other citizens of the former Soviet Union are very much aware of their nationality. Proud of their ethnicity, they are also curious about the national origins of persons they encounter. They will be pleased to tell foreign visitors about their own nationality, and visitors should not hesitate to ask.

RELIGION

A man who was not Orthodox could not be Russian.

—Dostoyevsky, *The Possessed*

Russian ethnicity, culture, and nationalism have been identified with Russian Orthodoxy, the state religion of Russia for more than 1,000 years. In every ethnic Russian there is an Orthodox heritage, and it can emerge when least expected. Dostoyevsky's dictum, however, would be challenged today by many Russians who do not profess Orthodoxy or any religion at all.

Russia had an estimated population of approximately 141 million in July 2008, but there is no reliable data that breaks down the population by religious belief. Available information, however, suggests that approximately 70 percent consider themselves to be Russian Orthodox Christians, although the vast majority of them are not regular churchgoers and regard Orthodoxy as an element in Russia's cultural and historical tradition. Muslims are the largest minority, with estimates ranging from 14 to 23 million, comprising up to perhaps 15 percent of the population. However, Muslim communities in the Volga-Urals region differ so much culturally and, in some cases, theologically from those in the Caucasus, that the two groups could be considered as separate communities. Protestants of various denominations are the second largest group of Christians, with more than two million followers. Catholics are estimated by the Catholic Church to number from 600,000 to 1.5 million, figures that also exceed Russian government estimates. Buddhists are estimated by the Buddhist Association of Russia to number between 1.5 to 2 million. Of Russia's Jews, an estimated 600,000 to one million remain, largely in Moscow and St .Petersburg, following large-scale emigration over the past two decades.[23]

Russian citizens with an Islamic heritage, although mostly secular, have become a growing concern to the Moscow government. In seven republics of the Russian Federation, Muslims are a majority, and their birth rate is higher than that of ethnic Russians. In Chechnya, rebels who began their rebellion with a focus on sovereignty or independence now identify with Muslim fundamentalism. And elsewhere in the Caucasus and in Central Asia, resurgent Islamic extremism worries governments there as well as in Moscow.

Religious belief among Russians, growing from year to year, is related to gender, age, and education. Women, the elderly, and those with incomplete secondary education rank more as believers than do other groups. However, growth in believers has also been seen among young people, men, and those with higher education. Rural residents are not significantly more religious than urban, but religious belief differs substantially between regions: more in the Trans-Volga heartland area of Russia, for example, and less in northwest Russia.

Despite their religious beliefs, Russians still reflect much of their pagan, pre-Christian past. A superstitious people, there are certain things they just do not do, and neither should visitors. Shaking hands across a threshold is believed to bring bad luck because, in traditional Russian folklore, the doorway is where the "house spirit" is believed to reside. Whistling indoors brings poverty. Sit at the corner of a table and you will never marry. And when you make a new purchase, you must drink to it or it will be lost, stolen, or vandalized. Many of these beliefs reflect fascination with the occult, which has been noted throughout Russian history and is now experiencing a revival.

Half of all Russians are said to believe in prophetic dreams and omens. Literature on astrology, palmistry, numerology, and the interpretation of dreams can be found in bookstores and sidewalk kiosks, and the interest in such subjects is not limited to common people. Mikhail Gorbachev's horoscope was published in a Moscow newspaper, Leonid Brezhnev was treated by a Georgian faith healer in his final years, and Boris Yeltsin had a team of Kremlin astrologers whose sole job was to help him make decisions.

Sorcery and witchcraft also have many believers in Russia. Newspapers advertise the services of clairvoyants, witches, and sorcerers. And in the *Duma* (parliament) elections of December 1999, astrologers were consulted by newspapers, businesspeople, and politicians seeking to ascertain the prospects of the various candidates. All this occurs in a country that has been Christian for more than 1,000 years but where the pagan past persists.

The origins of the Russian Church are in Byzantium, the Eastern branch of Christianity. Because of its Byzantine beginnings, the Russian Church regards itself as a direct descendant of the early Christian communities. From Byzantium also came the belief that Orthodox Christianity, as James Billington has written:

> had solved all the basic problems of belief and worship. All that was needed was "right praising" (the literal translation of *pravoslaviye*, the Russian version of the Greek *orthodoxos*) through forms of worship handed down by the Apostolic Church and defined for all time by its seven ecumenical councils. Changes in dogma or even sacred phraseology could not be tolerated, for there was but one answer to any controversy.[24]

The consensus of the Orthodox congregation was regarded as the truth—a singularity of truth in which there was no room for a pluralism of opinion. In this idea lie the roots of Russia's traditional disdain for dissidents, political as well as religious. The Russian word for dissident, *inakomyslyaschi,* actually means "a person who thinks differently."

Also with roots in Russian Orthodoxy is the Russian sense of community and egalitarianism. *Sobor,* the Russian word for *cathedral* (as well as *council*), indicates a coming together of congregants who share common Christian values. Stites describes sobor as signifying a "sense of harmonious spiritual community."[25]

Sobor is a symbolic word for Russians, who regard Roman Catholicism as too authoritarian and Protestantism as too individualistic. Catholicism is seen as authoritarian because each Catholic believer and each national church must submit to the authority of the Pope. Protestantism is too individualistic because each national church can make its own religious doctrine and can be further splintered from within. In Orthodoxy, by contrast, as Paul Miliukov put it, "A national authority could never conflict with the universal doctrine of the Eastern church, because the national churches had no power to introduce changes into the universal doctrine, and the universal doctrine had not been invested with power."[26]

Thus, while churches in the West labored vigorously to achieve independence in religious matters, in the East the creation of national churches came easily because there was no need to question religious doctrine, which, as noted by Billington earlier, had been defined for all time and was universally accepted. Russia was the first nation to have a national Orthodox church, and its example was followed by Greece, Georgia, Serbia, Romania, Bulgaria, and others. While autonomous, they are all members of the one Eastern church.

Russian Orthodoxy is also seen as egalitarian, a fellowship uniting all souls under a single and correct religious rite. The Orthodox vision of *sobornost* is described by Zernov as "the main driving force behind all the social and political endeavors of the Russian . . . the expression of the desire to treat their rapidly expanding state as one big family."[27] Among Orthodox Christians there is indeed a feeling of family.

Easter, the principal Russian religious holiday, has a special meaning for Russians, who become euphoric as their long and harsh winter comes to an end. For them, Easter signifies the resurrection of nature when, after six months of the immobility and death of winter, life suddenly returns to the land. Historically, the end of two centuries of Mongol rule is seen as a resurrection of the Russian people, achieved through their Christian faith.

At Easter, the Resurrection has its full meaning for Russians in Christ's victory over sin and death. "The service on Easter night," wrote Zernov, "is an experience which has no parallel in the worship of other nations. Only those who have been present at this service can realize all that the Resurrection means to the Russian people."[28] Visitors who are in Russia in the spring should be sure to attend an Easter service.

Under the Soviets, atheism became the official doctrine, and the Orthodox Church, with its tradition of submission to state authority—another legacy of Byzantium—proved easy to suppress and vulnerable to control. From a historical perspective, in old Russia there was one church, one truth, and little tolerance for dissidents. In the Soviet era—at least before 1985—the Communist Party replaced the Church, and Party ideology supplanted religious truth, while intolerance of dissidents greatly increased and became state policy.

As a substitute church, the Communist Party established a cult of Lenin, the founder and father of the Soviet state, and his portraits and busts became the icons of the new religion. Every school, workplace, and many homes had a *krasny ugol* (holy corner), in which an image of Lenin hung where religious icons had once been placed. And when Lenin died in 1924, he was embalmed and interred in a granite tomb next to the Kremlin, where his mummified remains still are on view to the public.

The spirit of Lenin, regarded by orthodox communists as immortal, was embodied in the popular slogan, "Lenin lived, Lenin lives, Lenin will live." And to remind Muscovites of Lenin's immortality, during the anniversary of the centennial of his birth in 1969 (which fell at Easter time), an image of Lenin was projected at night by searchlight onto a large balloon in the skies above the Kremlin. The significance of this event was not lost on Russians, who address each other at Easter with the traditional Orthodox greeting, "Christ has risen." Today Lenin no longer lives, but he still stands as a statue in the central square of many Russian provincial cities, and his followers have considerable support in rural areas and among pensioners, industrial workers, and members of former collective farms.

After 1985, the antireligious policies of the Stalin years were reversed. A law on freedom of conscience was passed in 1990, and Russians, responding to a rebirth of interest in Russian cultural traditions, are showing renewed interest in their Church.

Today about 70 percent of Russians are believers in Orthodoxy—though only a small proportion of those are regular church goers—and the Church is also supported by many nonbelievers who regard it as a symbol of Russian culture and an object of national pride. To endorse the renewed role of Orthodoxy in Russian life, and to confirm his cordial relationship with the Church, Prime Minister Putin has admitted to being baptized as a child and has openly asserted that he is a believer.

Russia in 2006 had more than 23,000 Orthodox parishes, more than triple the number in 1988, and more were being added despite the shortage of trained priests. Churches confiscated by the communists are being restored, and Moscow's imposing Cathedral of Christ the Savior, the world's largest Orthodox church, has been rebuilt overlooking the Moscow River, not far from the Kremlin. Built to commemorate Russia's victory over Napoleon in 1812, the church had been razed by Stalin in 1931 and replaced by a swimming pool. Religious institutions are again free to do charitable work, and the Church has also branched into business activities such as banking, hotels, and light manufacturing. Orthodox Christmas—which falls on January 7 under the old Julian calendar—is once more a state holiday, as it was prior to 1918. Orthodoxy is again a force in Russia. Moreover, it appears to be looking more and more like the state religion it once was, as robed priests give their blessings at major government and public events.

The role of the Russian Orthodox Church in post-Soviet Russia and worldwide was further enhanced on May 17, 2007, by the signing in Moscow of a canonical union between the Russian Orthodox Church and the Russian Orthodox Church Outside of Russia, also known as the Russian Church Abroad. The latter church was created in the 1920s by émigrés who had fled Russia after the civil war and the victory of the communists. Headquartered in New York City, and with nearly half of its 400 parishes in the United States, the church had long been a symbol of anticommunist and monarchist Russians in exile.

Foreign-based missionaries, many of them from Britain and the United States, are also now active in Russia despite efforts by the Orthodox Church to place restrictions on them. A law passed in 1997 threatened to jeopardize the status of the 17,000 non-Orthodox religious groups in Russia. The law exempted the four religious groups regarded as traditional—Christianity, Islam, Judaism, and Buddhism.

Under the law, groups not registered with the state—a difficult and time-consuming process—cannot own property or conduct public services. Among the religious groups affected by the law are certain Protestant,

Catholic, and Muslim congregations, as well as Scientologists, Jehovah's Witnesses, Hare Krishnas, and the Salvation Army. In September 2001, for example, a court shut down the Moscow chapter of the British-based Salvation Army, which runs soup kitchens for the poor and elderly. The city had charged that the Salvation Army had failed to register on time or prove its continued existence as the law requires. Moreover, since its members wear uniforms, they were accused by some of being part of a militarized force intent on overthrowing the Russian government.

The United States, in contrast to Russia, has had neither a state church, an official ideology, nor a single truth. Rather, it has known a pluralism of beliefs and truths, and it has tolerated, if not encouraged, dissenters from these truths. The country was settled initially by large numbers of religious and political dissidents from Europe who were more interested in worshiping God in their own way than in imposing their beliefs on others. Church and state have been kept separate, religion and ideology have been excluded from state affairs, and diverse views have been welcomed. Indeed, the very right to be different has been respected.

Americans have resisted universal systems of thought as well as ideologies that purport to have the answers to all questions and a grand plan for future action. If Americans do have an ideology, it is pragmatism—if it works, do it.

In Russia, however, creating a consensus, whether in religion or politics, has been seen as desirable, and dissidents viewed as somewhat strange—if not at times insane—for refusing to join it. According to Edward Keenan, director of the Dumbarton Oaks Research Library and Collection, Russians have a tendency to embrace a philosophical system that is not theirs to begin with and, after time, to proclaim themselves the sole custodians of its true interpretation.[29]

THREE

Culture and Character

The Russian is a delightful person till he tucks in his shirt. As an oriental he is charming. It is only when he insists upon being treated as the most easterly of western peoples instead of the most westerly of easterns that he becomes a racial anomaly and extremely difficult to handle. The host never knows which side of his nature is going to turn up next.

—Rudyard Kipling, *The Man Who Was*

EGALITARIANISM

The interests of distribution and egalitarianism always predominated over those of production and creativity in the minds and emotions of the Russian intelligentsia.

—Nikolai Berdiaev, in *Vekhi*

Americans are raised on the success ethic—work hard, get ahead, be successful in whatever you do. The success ethic, however, is alien to many Russians, who believe that it may be morally wrong to get ahead, particularly at the expense of others. Russians will not mind if their American acquaintances are successful, but they are likely to resent fellow Russians who "succeed." Belief in communism has eroded, but the egalitarian ethic still survives.

"In Russia," writes Nina Khrushcheva,

"equality of outcomes," a belief that material conditions in society should not vary too greatly among individual and classes, wins out over Western "equality of opportunities," which tends to tolerate and even encourage the open flourishing of class distinctions. Therefore, working for money, for example, a virtue so respected in the West, was not a "good way" in Russia. Russians can be great workers, as long as labor is done not for profit but for some spiritual or personal reason or is done as a heroic deed, performing wonders, knowing no limits.[30]

Egalitarianism is a social philosophy that advocates the removal of inequities among persons and a more equal distribution of benefits. In its Russian form egalitarianism is not an invention of communists but has its roots in the culture of the mir which, as we have seen, represented village democracy, Russian-style.

The mir's governing body was an assembly composed of heads of households, including widowed women, and presided over by a *starosta* (elder). Before the introduction of currency, mir members were economically equal, and equality for members was considered more important than personal freedom. Those agricultural communes, with their egalitarian lifestyle and distribution of material benefits, were seen by Russian intellectuals as necessary to protect the peasants from the harsh competition of Western individualism. Individual rights, it was feared, would enable the strong to prosper but cause the weak to suffer. Others saw the mir as a form of agrarian socialism, the answer to Russia's striving for egalitarianism.

For much of Russian history, peasants numbered close to 90 percent of the population. By 1990, however, due to industrialization, the figure had dropped to about 30 percent. But while the other 70 percent of the population live in urban areas, most of today's city dwellers are only one, two, or three generations removed from their ancestral villages. Despite their urbanization and education, the peasant past is still very much with them, and many of them still think in the egalitarian terms of the mir.

The Soviet state also thought in egalitarian terms. Communism aimed to make a complete break with the past and create a new society, but its leaders could not escape the heritage of the past, and their leveling of society revived the communal ethic of the mir on a national scale. As British scholar Geoffrey Hosking observed:

In some ways . . . the Soviet state has perpetuated the attitudes of the pre-1930 Russian village community. The expectation is still prevalent that the community will guarantee essentials in a context of comradely indigence just above the poverty line.[31]

Many aspects of Russian communism may indeed be traced to the mir. The meetings of the village assembly were lively, but decisions were usually unanimous and binding on all members. This provided a precedent for the communism's "democratic centralism," under which issues were debated, decisions were made that all Party members were obliged to support, and opposition was prohibited.

Peasants could not leave the mir without an internal passport issued only with permission of their household head. This requirement was a precursor not only of Soviet (and tsarist) regulations denying citizens freedom of movement and resettlement within the country, but also of the practice of denying emigration to those who did not have parental permission. Under communism, the tapping of telephones and the perusal of private mail by the KGB must have seemed natural to leaders whose ancestors lived in a mir where the community was privy to the personal affairs of its members. And in a society where the bulk of the population was tied to the land and restricted in movement, defections by Soviet citizens abroad were seen as treasonous.

Despite its egalitarian ethic, old Russia also had an entrepreneurial tradition based in a small merchant class called *kupyechestvo*. Russian merchants established medieval trading centers, such as the city-state of Novgorod, which were independent and self-governing until absorbed by Muscovy in the late fifteenth century. Merchants explored and developed Siberia and played a key role in Russia's industrialization of the late nineteenth and early twentieth centuries.

Merchants were also Westernizers in the years between the revolutions of 1905 and 1917, endorsing social and legal reform, the rule of law, civil liberties, and broader educational opportunities. However, they rejected economic liberalism, with its emphasis on free trade in international exchange and free competition in the domestic economy, and advocated instead state planning. And as an additional link in the chain of continuity between the old and new Russia, as Ruth Roosa has pointed out, merchants in the years prior to 1917 called for state plans of 5, 10, and even 15 years' duration that would embrace all aspects of economic life.[32]

Agriculture in old Russia also had its entrepreneurs. Most of the land was held in large estates by the crown, aristocracy, and landed gentry, but after the emancipation of the serfs in 1861, a small class of independent farmers emerged. By 1917, on the eve of the Revolution, some 10 percent of the peasants were independent farmers. The more enterprising and prosperous among them were called *kulaks* (fists) by their less successful and envious brethren who had remained in the mir. But the kulaks were ruthlessly exterminated and their land forcibly collectivized by the communists in the early 1930s. Millions of peasants left the land they had farmed, production was disrupted, and more than five million died in the resulting famine. The forced collectivization contributed to the eventual failure of Soviet agriculture.

Private farming returned to Russia in the late 1980s and grew steadily over the following years, encouraged by Mikhail Gorbachev's perestroika, legislation passed by the Russian parliament, and decrees issued by Boris Yeltsin. The legal underpinning for agricultural reform was provided by Article 36 of the new Russian constitution, approved by the electorate in December 1993, which affirmed that "Citizens and their associations shall be entitled to have land in private ownership." Parliament, however, reflecting historic attitudes on communal ownership of land, balked at passing legislation that would have put that article into effect.[33] The opposition in parliament was led by the Communist and Agrarian Parties, and most land remained government property, as it was during Soviet times when Communist ideology required that the state own the means of production.

That changed on October 26, 2001, when Vladimir Putin, drawing to close a decade of efforts by Russia's leadership to ease Soviet-era land sale restrictions, put his pen to legislation giving Russians the right to purchase land. However, the new land code affected only some 2 percent of Russian land, and it covered purchases only for industrial, urban housing, and recreational purposes, but not for farmland. Another law, passed in 2003, finally granted rights to private ownership of land and the possibility for sale and purchase of agricultural land.

However, opposition to private land ownership is still strong. Opponents of farmland sales, in addition to their ideological misgivings, believe that such sales will open the way for wealthy Russians and foreign investors to buy up large tracts of land. Foreigners have the right to buy commercial and residential land but not farmland, although long-term leases by foreigners are permitted. Supporters of farmland sales believe this will further Russia's transition to a market economy, encourage foreign investment, improve agricultural productivity, promote growth of a property-owning class, provide revenue by taxing privately owned land, and curb the corruption that has facilitated illegal land transactions.

Despite all the supportive legislation and decrees, private agriculture is still not widely accepted by Russian peasants, most of whom oppose reform and are reluctant to leave the security of the former collective and state farms for the risks of the free market.[34] Impediments to private farming include difficulties in acquiring enough land and equipment to start a farm, a general lack of credit, the reluctance of peasants to give up the broad range of social services provided by the collective and state farms, and a fear that if land reform is reversed they will once more be branded as kulaks and will lose their land.

Despite its vastness, Russia has relatively little area suited for agriculture because of its arid climate and inconsistent rainfall. Northern areas concentrate mainly on livestock, and southern parts and western Siberia produce grain. Restructuring of former state farms has been a slow process. Nevertheless, private farms and individual garden plots account for over one-half of all agricultural production.[35]

Economic reforms have also been slow to gain support among the general public, particularly with the older generation. While there is a streak of individualism in many Russians, the entrepreneurial spirit of the businessperson and independent farmer runs counter to Russian egalitarianism. For many Russians, selling goods for profit is regarded as dishonest and is called *spekulatsiya* (speculation). Russians, it has been said, would rather bring other people down to their level than try to rise higher, a mentality known as *uravnilovka* (leveling). As Vladimir Shlapentokh, a professor at Michigan State University, points out:

> Indeed, the traditional political culture and Orthodox religion were always hostile toward rich people. Ever since the time of Alexander Radishchev, one would be hard pressed to find a single Russian writer who imparted sentiments with even an inkling of admiration for wealth and the privileged lifestyle. It suffices to mention the giants of the Russian literary tradition, such as Gogol, Turgenev, Dostoevsky, Tolstoy and, of course, Maxim Gorky.[36]

CAUTION AND CONSERVATISM

The slower you go, the further you'll get.

—Russian proverb

Living in a country that claimed to be socialist, Russians were assumed by many in the West to be radicals and challengers of the established order. In reality, they are more likely to be cautious and conservative defenders of the status quo—and with good reason. Their cruel climate, harsh history, and skeptical outlook on life have caused Russians to value stability, security, social order, and predictability and to avoid risk. Big changes are feared, and the tried and tested is preferred over the new and unknown.

Caution and conservatism are also legacies of the peasant past. Barely eking out a living in small isolated villages, peasants had to contend not only with the vagaries of nature but also with the strictures of communal life, authoritarian fathers, all-powerful officials, and reproachful religious leaders. In a traditional agricultural society, stability was valued and change came slowly. As Marshall Shulman of Columbia University once put it, "Russians feel obliged to defend their traditional values against the onslaught of the modern world."[37]

The experience of the twentieth century has given Russians no cause to discard their caution. "Man-made catastrophes," writes Stephen F. Cohen of New York University, "have repeatedly victimized millions of ordinary [Russian] citizens and officials alike—the first European war, revolution, civil war, two great famines, forced collectivization, Stalin's terror, World War II, and more." From those events, concludes Cohen, has come a conservatism that is "a real bond between state and society—and thus the main obstacle to change."[38]

Caution and conservatism can also be seen at the highest levels of government, where most of the leadership has been of peasant origin. Reflecting their peasant past, Russia's leaders will take advantage of every opportunity to advance their cause but will be careful to avoid undue risk.

The cautious approach was recommended by Mikhail Gorbachev in a talk in Washington during his June 1990 summit meeting with President George H. W. Bush. Noting that he preferred not to act precipitously in resolving international differences, Gorbachev advocated an approach that "is more humane. That is, to be very cautious, to consider a matter seven times, or even 100 times before one makes a decision."[39]

Boris Yeltsin was also overly cautious when it was in his interest and Russia's to be bold and daring. In June 1991, when he enjoyed high prestige and popularity after his election as president, and in August of that year after he foiled an attempted coup, Yeltsin's caution prevented him from instituting the broad reforms that Russia required. As for Putin, if there is one word to describe him it is *cautious*. Andrew Jack, former Moscow bureau chief of London's *Financial Times*, describes Putin as a cautious president who is very hard to categorize:

> A Teflon personality designed to draw out his interlocutors without revealing much about himself, saying what they wanted to hear and promising what they sought, while not necessarily believing or planning to implement it.[40]

Some speak of a congenital Russian inertia. As an old Russian proverb puts it, "The Russian won't budge until the roasted rooster pecks him in the rear."

Americans will have their patience tested by Russian caution. A nation of risk takers, most Americans are descendants of immigrants who dared to leave the known of the Old World for the unknown of the New. In the United States, risk takers have had the opportunity to succeed or to fail in the attempt. Indeed, risk is the quintessence of a market economy. The opportunities of the New World, with its social mobility and stability, have helped Americans to accentuate the positive. For Russians, geography and history have caused them to anticipate the negative.

PESSIMISM

We did the best we could, but it turned out as usual.
> —Viktor Chernomyrdin, former Russian prime minister

Russian pessimism is the source of many *anekdoti* (as Russian jokes are called). According to one, pessimists say, "Things can't be worse than they are now." Optimists say, "Yes they can." Another anekdot describes a Russian pessimist as a realistic optimist. Foreign business representatives will have to become realistic optimists themselves in appraising prospects for their ventures in Russia.

Russian pessimism contrasts with American innocence and optimism. Americans expect things to go well, and they become annoyed when they do not. Russians expect things to go poorly and have learned to live with disappointments.

Americans, for example, like happy endings in their horoscopes as well as in their novels and films. Russians astrologers and writers spin tales of tragedy. American horoscopes are generally upbeat, with such advice as "You'll breathe the fresh air of freedom. Everything seems to be going your way. You are very original; there is no one else like you. Your finances will be better than anticipated." Russian horoscopes, by contrast, are full of gloom and doom, advising, "This month will bring the loss of friends and protectors, and hostility and deceit. All attempts to interfere with the natural course of events and to change it for the better will lead to no good results. You should not expect anything good from your family life today. Don't be frantic when you learn that all your savings are gone."

The pessimism of astrologers, however, apparently does not apply to their horoscopes for the nation. In a 2001 end-of-the-year press conference, Russia's most prominent astrologist, Pavel Globa, predicted that the year 2002 would be very successful for Russia. Political and economic developments would be positive, he said, reforms would continue, there would be no crises, and after crucial changes in the coming year, Russia would again be a superpower.[41] And, with the exception of the attack by Chechen militants on a Moscow theater in which more than 100 hostages died, the astrologer was right. Globa, however, failed to predict the future of his marriage to another astrologer, which ended in divorce.

Putting astrologers' predictions aside, life has indeed been difficult for Russians. Weather, wars, violence, cataclysmic changes, and oppressive rule over centuries have made pessimists of them. Russians have a "gloom-and-doom mentality," writes U.S. translator and writer Richard Lourie. "Both at the kitchen table and in print, they indulge in apocalyptic prophecies."[42]

When asked to explain the grounds for his pessimism, a Russian professor told me, "Our main concern, that which determines all our actions and feelings, is *strakh* (fear). The world is dangerous, and we must be careful."

Fear is a major element of the Russian psyche, and strakh will be encountered in many places in Russia, even at the highest levels of government, where there is often fear of an outside enemy determined to destroy Russia. Americans should not be put off by this gloom and doom, nor should they attempt to make optimists of Russians. The best response is to express understanding and sympathy.

When asked how things are, a Russian is likely to reply *normalno* (normal), which might be translated as "not too bad." Translators Richard Lourie and Aleksei Mikhalev go further, describing normalno as "a wistful, ironic word, containing all the pain that came before and all of the hope of what might yet come to pass, the great dream of the present, a 'normal' society."[43]

Less in control of their lives than other Europeans and Americans, Russians feel caught up in the big sweeps of history where the individual is insignificant and does not count. As Lourie and Mikhalev explain, the difference is simple and dramatic:

> For us, history is a subject, a black-and-white newsreel; for them it is a tank on their street, a search of their apartment by strangers with power. . . . Nearly every life has been touched directly, branded, by the great historical spasms of revolution, war and terror. For a Russian, repression always comes from the outside world. . . .[44]

Glasnost and perestroika were exciting for foreigners to observe from a distance, but to Russians they were yet another historical spasm with attendant uncertainties about the future. Today many Russians see their country threatened by ethnic warfare and environmental degradation. Some Russians even speak of genetic degradation.

The best and brightest have traditionally been banished. In old Russia independent thinkers were exiled to Siberia. Following the Bolshevik Revolution, the cream of Russia's elite was liquidated. Stalin's purges of the 1930s further decimated the intelligentsia, and today many of Russia's best and brightest have been lost through emigration.

One of those who emigrated is Vladimir Voinovich, a popular and critically acclaimed writer and human rights advocate who was forced to leave for the West in 1975 after the KGB suggested to him that his future in the Soviet Union would be "unbearable." A satirist in the tradition of Gogol, Voinovich has described how Americans and Russians react differently to his writing. "Russians and Americans," he writes, "read my books in very different ways. Americans usually say they are funny. Russians say . . . they are very gloomy, dark."[45] This gloomy and dark side of the Russian character explains the bittersweet humor that is native to Russia and the "good news, bad news" jokes. (Voinovich returned to Russia in 1990, and spends most of his time there.)

Russian pessimism can also be infectious, and Americans who have worked with them for many years are vulnerable to the virus. Llewellyn Thompson, twice American ambassador to Moscow, was asked on his retirement in 1968 to name his greatest accomplishment. "That I didn't make things any worse," replied the veteran diplomat.[46]

Despite their pessimism and complaining, there is an admirable durability about Russians, a hardy people who have more than proven their ability to endure severe deprivation and suffer lengthy hardships. Tibor Szamuely has written of "the astonishing durability of . . . certain key social and political institutions, traditions, habits, and attitudes, their staying power, their essential stability amidst the turbulent currents of violent change, chaotic upheaval, and sudden innovation."[47]

Russian pessimism, however, may be slowly giving way to optimism. Recent public opinion polls show that half of all Russians now say that things have changed for the better. Younger people have only distant memories of the Soviet years. As one pollster put it:

> Over the past three or four years, Russian citizens have been able to plan their lives further ahead. In other words, success-oriented people have come to believe that their personal future can be better than the present, and that they can plan to be better off than they are.[48]

Will the trend toward optimism continue? Watch the price of oil and gas.

EXTREMES AND CONTRADICTIONS

Contradiction is . . . the essence of Russia. West and East, Pacific and Atlantic, Arctic and tropics, extreme cold and extreme heat, prolonged sloth and sudden feats of energy, exaggerated cruelty and exaggerated kindness, ostentatious wealth and dismal squalor, violent xenophobia and uncontrollable yearning for contact with the foreign world, vast power and the most abject slavery, simultaneous love and hate for the same objects. . . . The Russian does not reject these contradictions. He has learned to live with them, and in them. To him, they are the spice of life.

—George F. Kennan, *Memoirs*

President Harry Truman once quipped that he was looking for a one-armed economist because all his economic advisers concluded their advice by saying, "But, on the other hand. . . ." Americans, with their proclivity for rational consistency seek clear and precise responses, but they usually end up by falling back to a middle position that avoids contradictions and extremes.

Russians, by contrast, have a well-deserved reputation for extremes. When emotions are displayed, they are spontaneous and strong. Russian hospitality can be overwhelming, friendship all encompassing, compassion deep, loyalty long lasting, drinking heavy, celebrations boisterous, obsession with security paranoid, and violence vicious. With Russians, it is often all or nothing. Halfway measures simply do not suffice.

"The Anglo-Saxon instinct," wrote George F. Kennan, distinguished U.S. diplomatist and historian, "is to attempt to smooth away contradictions, to reconcile opposing elements, to achieve something in the nature of an acceptable middle ground as a basis for life." The Russian, continued Kennan, tends to deal only in extremes, "and he is not particularly concerned to reconcile them."[49] The American mind, concluded Kennan, will not understand Russia until it accepts that

> because a proposition is true, the opposite of that proposition is not false. It must agree never to entertain a proposition about the Russian world without seeking, and placing in apposition to it, its inevitable and indispensable opposite. Then it must agree to regard both as legitimate, valid conceptions . . . to understand that Russian life at any given moment is not the common expression of harmonious integrated elements, but a precarious and evershifting equilibrium between numbers of conflicting forces. . . . Right and wrong, reality and unreality, are determined in Russia, not by any God, not by any innate nature of things, but simply by men themselves. Here men determine what is true and what is false.[50]

Russian extremes and contradictions have also been described by poet Yevgeny Yevtushenko:

> I am thus and not thus, I am industrious and lazy, determined and shiftless. I am . . . shy and impudent, wicked and good; in me is a mixture of everything from the west to the east, from enthusiasm to envy. . . .[51]

Human feelings count for much in Russia, and those who do not share the depth of those feelings will be considered cold and distant. When Russians open their souls to someone, it is a sign of acceptance and sharing. Westerners will have to learn to drop their stiff upper lips and also open their souls.

THE RUSSIAN SOUL

The famous "Russian soul" was to no small extent the product of this agonizing uncertainty regarding Russia's proper geographical, social, and spiritual position in the world, the awareness of a national personality that was split between East and West.

—Tibor Szamuely, *The Russian Tradition*

Andrei Amalryk, the political dissident I used to visit in the small room he shared with his wife in a Moscow communal apartment, was in trouble with the Soviet authorities for most of his adult life. During his sentence to political exile in faraway Magadan, just across the Bering Strait from Alaska, Amalryk encountered by chance the man who had denounced him to the authorities. The denouncer expressed regret, asked forgiveness, and suggested they have a drink. After consuming a bottle of vodka—which got both of them drunk—the denouncer became even more remorseful and asked Amalryk what he could do to make amends. Amalryk suggested that he write an account of what he had done. The denouncer wrote out a confession of how he had succumbed to KGB pressure and falsified his testimony, signed it, and presented it to Amalryk with deep emotion. A few hours later, however, sober and no longer remorseful, he asked that it be returned to him and, when Amalryk refused, even offered to buy it back.[52]

Russkaya dusha (Russian soul) can turn up suddenly in the most unexpected places—and just as suddenly disappear. Just when foreigners believe that Russians are about to get down to serious business, they can become decidedly emotional and unbusinesslike.

Dusha is well known in the arts, where it manifests itself as emotion, sentimentality, exuberance, energy, theatricality, flamboyant virtuosity, and bravura technique. Dusha, however, transcends the arts and is the essence of Russian behavior. A romantic ethos, dusha appeals to feeling rather than fact, sentiment over certainty, suffering instead of satisfaction, and nostalgia for the past as opposed to the reality of the present. In a broader sense, dusha is also a reaffirmation of the purity of traditional Russian values against the encroachment of Western enlightenment, rationalism, and secularism, especially in things cultural.

Russian dusha is often derided in the West as a fantasy of artists, composers, and writers. If dusha ever really existed, this argument goes, it was the product of a traditional agricultural society that had very little in material goods to offer. In a modern industrial society, the argument continues, dusha is quickly forgotten and Russians become as realistic, practical, materialistic, and unromantic as Westerners.

The truth, as in many things Russian, lies somewhere in between. Russians do have a rich spirituality that does indeed contrast with Western rationalism, materialism, and pragmatism. Russians suffer but seem to enjoy their suffering. Obsessed with ideas, their conversation is weighty and lengthy. The rational and pragmatic approach does not always work for them. More often, it is personal relations, feelings, and traditional values that determine a course of action. Westerners are more likely to depend on the cold facts and to do what works.

As Tatyana Tolstaya, one of Russia's leading contemporary writers, says:

> Logical categories are inapplicable to the soul. But Russian sensitivity, permeating the whole culture, doesn't want to use logic—logic is seen as dry and evil, logic comes from the devil—the most important thing is sensation, smell, emotion, tears, mist, dreams, and enigma.[53]

"In Russian culture, emotion is assigned an entirely positive value," writes Tolstaya. "The more a person expresses his emotions, the better, more sincere, and more 'open' he is."[54] The Russian mentality, she believes, has penetrated to some degree all corners of the country, but "often not for the best." Dusha is described by Tolstaya as

> sensitivity, reverie, imagination, an inclination to tears, compassion, submission mingled with stubbornness, patience that permits survival in what would seem to be unbearable circumstances, poetry, mysticism, fatalism, a penchant for walking the dark, humid back streets of consciousness, introspection, sudden, unmotivated cruelty, mistrust of rational thought, fascination with the word—the list could go on and on—all these qualities that have frequently been attributed to the "Slavic soul."[55]

That Slavic soul, however, also has many aspects that Westerners can respect and admire. As Northwestern University professor Irwin Weil puts it:

> Russians maintain their integrity in a way that conforms to their inner notion of what a human being should be, in a manner they consider proper, and with an honesty and decency that I have seldom seen anywhere else in the world. Above all, they have an appreciation for *tselnost* (wholeness, complete commitment) and faith, no matter what that faith may be related to. To be a real human being, one must maintain that full commitment, and respect it in other people as well. In this sense, it makes no difference to them whether the other person is a Marxist or a reactionary.[56]

Russians are sensitive to the feelings of others as well as their own. Weil recalls how, while he was an exchange student at Moscow State University during the Cuban missile crisis of 1962, Cuban students placed signs above the doors to their dormitory rooms calling President Kennedy an s.o.b. Russian students complained to the student council that the signs were offensive to American students at the university, and the student council ordered that they be removed. On the death of President Kennedy in 1963, Weil received three letters from Russian friends expressing their personal condolences.[57] And, in 2001, after the World Trade Center disaster in New York, I received many similar messages of condolence from Russian friends and acquaintances.

Other examples of Russian soul are the courage and moral strength of the Soviet Union's two most prominent political dissidents, Andrei Sakharov and Aleksandr Solzhenitsyn, in the face of KGB harassment and persecution. Their politics differed—Sakharov was a Westernizer and Solzhenitsyn a Slavophile—but both were awarded Nobel Prizes, the former for peace, the latter for literature.

Sakharov, the celebrated nuclear physicist who helped to develop the Soviet hydrogen bomb, suffered seven years of internal exile in Gorky (now Nizhny Novgorod) for his outspoken opposition to the Soviet war in Afghanistan. Returning to Moscow in 1986, ailing but unbroken in spirit, one year after Gorbachev's coming to power, he continued his struggle for human rights and led the democratic opposition until his untimely death in 1989.

Solzhenitsyn, after a search of his house by the KGB in 1971, during which one of his friends was brutally beaten, had the courage to send an indignant open letter of protest to Yuri Andropov, head of the KGB at the time. In his letter, Solzhenitsyn demanded from Andropov "the public identification of all the intruders, their punishment as criminals, and a public explanation of this incident. Otherwise I can only conclude that they were sent by you."[58] Solzhenitsyn, author of *The Gulag Archipelago*, an exposé of Stalin's slave labor camps, survived his challenge to the KGB but was exiled from the Soviet Union in 1974. After 20 years of exile in Vermont, he returned to Russia in 1994, where he died in 2008.

In the early years of the twenty-first century, the Russian soul is still spirited. Old virtues endure—respect for parents, deference to old age, regard for learning. Belief in village virtues is still strong—self-sacrifice, sense of duty, compassion, importance of family, love of nature. These aspects of the Russian soul are again the themes of "village writers," as they are known, who glorify peasant life and encourage a renaissance of traditional Russian values. Students hang on the words of their professors. Grateful audiences present flowers to musical and theatrical performers. Before vacating a home where they have lived for some time, Russians will sit quietly for a minute or two, reflecting on the events they have experienced there. Even in the post-industrial age, Russians demonstrate that emotions and personal feelings still matter.

But today, fear for the future of the Russian soul bothers Russians. Their dusha has survived centuries of church and state domination and 70 years of communism. Will it also survive, they wonder, the transition to the free market and democracy, and the call of Western culture?

BIG IS BEAUTIFUL

In its grandiose schemes, which were always on a worldwide scale, communism makes use of the Russian disposition for making plans and castle-building, which had hitherto no scope for practical application.

—Nikolai Berdiaev, *The Origin of Russian Communism*

"Sire, every thing is done on a large scale in this country—every thing is colossal."[59] So spoke the Marquis de Custine, addressing Tsar Nicholas in St. Petersburg in 1839 at the start of his travels through Russia. The French aristocrat was moved by the grand scale of "this colossal empire," as he described it in his four-volume *Russia in 1839*.

Modern-day travelers to Russia will also encounter colossal sights. In Moscow's Kremlin, guides point with pride to the Tsar Cannon—cast in 1586, with a bore of 36 inches and weight of 44 tons. Nearby is the Tsar Bell—20 feet high and, at 200 tons, the heaviest bell in the world.

Soviet leaders continued that "colossalism." When they industrialized, centralizing production to achieve economies of scale, they built gigantic industrial complexes employing up to 100,000 workers. *Gigantomania* is the term used by Western economists to describe that phenomenon. The Palace of Soviets, a Stalin project of the 1930s, was to have been the tallest building in the world, dwarfing the Empire State Building and the Eiffel Tower, and be topped by a 230-foot statue of Lenin. The Kremlin's Palace of Congresses, the huge hall known to Western TV viewers as the site of mass meetings, seats 6,000 and is one of the world's largest conference halls. Its snack bar can feed 3,000 people in 10 minutes, thanks to the many Russian grandmothers who staff its *bufet*.

In Volgograd (formerly Stalingrad), the site of a decisive battle with Germany in World War II, a victorious Mother Russia, the largest full-figure statue in the world, towers 282 feet over the battlefield. And Russia's new victory monument to World War II, completed in 1995, is 465 feet high and topped by a 27-ton Nike, the goddess of victory.

Aeroflot was by far the world's largest airline, flying abroad as well as to the far corners of the Soviet Union. Its supersonic transport (SST), the world's first, was considerably larger than the Anglo-French Concorde. And when McDonald's opened its first hamburger restaurant in Moscow in 1990—on Pushkin Square, only a few blocks from the Kremlin—it was the largest McDonald's in the world, with 26 cash registers and a capacity of 900 customers, and it broke McDonald's worldwide opening day records for customers served. By 2008, the Pushkin Square McDonald's was the second busiest in the world, and McDonald's more than 200 restaurants in Russia were serving more than 200,000 customers a day. That's a lot of *gamburgers* as the Russians call them (the German/English *h* is rendered in Russian as *g*).

Russians are impressed with size and numbers, and much that they do is on a grandiose scale. That is not unusual for a vast country. Russians think and act big, and they do not do things in a half-hearted way. Nor are these traits uniquely Russian. Americans, accustomed to wide open spaces and with an expansive outlook on life, also are known to think big.

Big also describes the Russian military. Even after large reductions, the Russian military in 2008 had more than one million personnel under arms. It also had the biggest missiles, submarines, and aircraft, and their numerical superiority over most U.S. equivalents has been used by the Pentagon in the past to justify requests for larger military budgets.[60]

To be sure, the United States has to consider foreign capabilities in determining the forces needed to counter them. But when motives were sought for Russian advantages in conventional forces, all possibilities should have been considered. Did they need such large forces to defend their vast territory and long borders? Did they seek quantitative superiority to counter a U.S. qualitative lead? Did they build big because they did not have the technology to build small? Those were possible explanations that should have been considered in analyzing Russian motives. Another explanation, however, is simply that Russians are impressed with size and numbers. For Russians, big is beautiful.

Russia's grandiose plans have at times been realized but at other times not. The Tsar Bell was too heavy and was neither hung nor rung. The Tsar Cannon was too big to fire. The Palace of Soviets was abandoned after the foundation proved incapable of supporting the huge structure, and the site was used for an outdoor swimming pool—one of the largest in Europe, of course. The Soviet SST had major design problems and was shelved after several crashes, including one at the prestigious Paris Air Show. Aeroflot's extensive domestic network was broken up into nearly 400 separate companies, with a drastic decline in safety standards. Russia's huge industrial plants have proven to be highly inefficient and noncompetitive, and the large state subsidies they require to avoid bankruptcy are an obstacle to their privatization. The Russian army's combat capabilities, as confirmed in the Chechnya war, have dramatically declined. And the *Kursk,* pride of the Russian navy and one of the largest submarines ever built, suffered an unexplained explosion in August 2000, and sank to the bottom of the Barents Sea with the loss of its entire crew of 118.

Russians, however, still have grand designs. In April 2007, Russia announced the revival of an old plan from its tsarist years to build a tunnel under the Bering Sea that would link Siberia with Alaska. And what should be said of Moscow's current politics, the most recent of many attempts to reform Russia? The objective this time is to modernize Russia, to make it more competitive with the West, and to regain its superpower status.

Will the sweeping reforms succeed or are they merely the latest example of Russians thinking too big? History tells us to believe the latter. As Anton Chekhov put it 100 years ago, "A Russian is particularly given to exalted ideas, but why is it he always falls so short in life? Why?"[61]

WOMEN—THE STRONGER SEX

Oh, Russian women, draft horses of the nation!

—Andrei Sinyavsky, *Goodnight!*

Some countries are called a fatherland, others a motherland. Russia is clearly a motherland. *Rodina,* the Russian word for "homeland," is feminine, and Mother Russia is the symbol of the nation. In this motherland, women are strong, hardworking, nurturing, long suffering, and the true heroes of Russia. They hold the country together.

Russian literature, writes British scholar Ronald Hingley, again and again gives us situations

> in which a beautiful, strong, well-integrated, decisive young woman becomes erotically implicated with some spineless, dithering pipsqueak of a man who invariably emerges discredited from the involvement. In fiction of the totalitarian [Soviet] period the clash between strong female and

weak male is more than ever in vogue, and has been well analyzed in terms which appropriately recall the life-cycle of the spider.[62]

The Bolsheviks professed to liberate women and give them full equality with men, and in the 1920s Soviet women enjoyed an equality under law unequaled anywhere else in the world. On this point Soviet law was explicit. As Article 35 of the 1977 Soviet Constitution declared:

> Women and men have equal rights in the USSR . . . ensured by according women equal access with men to education and vocational and professional training, equal opportunities in employment, remuneration and promotion, and in social and political and cultural activity.[63]

In practice, however, women were recognized but unrewarded. A state that claimed to have given all power to the people did in fact give power to only a few, and almost all of them were men.

During the entire Soviet era, only three women were named to the ruling Politburo of the Communist Party, and almost none were appointed to high positions in the military and diplomatic corps. To be sure, the first woman ambassador of any country was an early Bolshevik, Aleksandra Kollontai, who was named Soviet Minister to Norway in 1923—but only after her ardent feminism and advocacy of free love put her on a collision course with Party leaders at home.

Women worked in factories and on farms to help build the Soviet economy, and they fought in World War II. The Soviet air force had three air groups "manned" entirely by women, flying bombers by night, dive bombers by day, and even fighter planes. Together, they flew more than 30,000 combat missions during World War II. One woman pilot, Lilya Litvak, had 12 "kills," making her an ace before she was shot down and died at age 22.

In the new Russia, equal rights for women and men have been reaffirmed by Article 19 of the Constitution of 1993, which asserts, "The state shall guarantee equal human and civil rights and freedoms without regard to sex. . . . Men and women shall have equal rights and freedoms and equal opportunities to exercise them."[64] In practice, however, the results differ.

Some 62 percent of Russian women are college graduates, compared to 50 percent of men, but the average woman's salary is one-third smaller than that of men.[65] The majority of middle- and high-ranking professionals are women, and Russia has one of the highest rates of women bosses. But while more than 80 percent of school principals are women, they comprise only

6 percent of rectors (presidents) of universities and other higher schools, and women make up only 8 percent of high-ranking officials. In cutbacks, women are the first to be fired, but they are quick learners of new professions and bolder in business, and they head about 30 percent of medium-sized businesses and 10 percent of big businesses.

Women, who outnumber men by 10 million, are active today in all professions and occupations, but they are especially strong in medicine where, reflecting an old Russian tradition, three-fourths of all medical doctors are women. They also predominate in teaching and in the textile, food, and social service industries. But while few women occupy high government positions, they have been active in recent years in establishing a broad range of public and political organizations in the new civil society of Russia. Women are also becoming more active in business, founding and directing their own firms, and in journalism.

Women actually work two shifts—one at the workplace and the other at home, where they put in another full workweek performing the duties of wife, mother, and homemaker. Moreover, as Russian society becomes more consumer-oriented, men work longer hours to earn more and now do an even smaller share of the household tasks than before.

Sexual harassment in the workplace is common, as is wife beating at home. According to official statistics, 14,000 Russian women are killed each year by their husbands and boyfriends, and 38,000 are beaten daily.[66] Police generally take a hands-off attitude, and women do not know their rights in a country that still seems to believe a popular Russian adage, "If he beats you, it means that he loves you."

"The Russian woman—and this is proven by research—is more capable of love than Europeans and Americans," says psychotherapist and sexologist professor Aleksandr Poleyev. "Passions of Russian women last longer, and dependence on love is a characteristic of Russian women." He adds, however, that patriarchal prejudice and taboo affect the sex life of Russian women, and 33 percent are not satisfied with their sex life.[67] (It is not stated where or how Poleyev did his research.)

Gorbachev, in his book *Perestroika*, said it was imperative to involve women more in the management of the economy, cultural development, and public life, and to promote them to administrative posts. However, when discussing problems caused by weakened family ties, Gorbachev noted that heated debates are being held "about the question of what we should do to make it possible for women to return to their purely womanly mission."[68]

That "purely womanly mission" has been frustrated by recent history. Forty million Soviet men died in the three cataclysmic events of the Soviet era—the collectivization of agriculture, the political purges, and World War II—creating a severe shortage of men for two generations of women. Moreover, the mortality rate for Russian men today is four times that of women in all age groups over twenty due to alcoholism and related accidents and illnesses, and women outlive men, on average, by thirteen years.[69] That explains why there are so many *babushki* (grandmothers) in Russia and so few *dyedushki* (grandfathers).

Attitudes on birth control stem from traditional Russian conservatism as well as the views of a male-dominated leadership, which has sought to stabilize the family and increase the birthrate. Most families, however, avoid having a second child due to limited housing (especially in the cities), a decline in state-subsidized day care, the collapse of the state welfare system, and the deterioration of health care, as well as the increased cost of living. The use of contraceptives, now more available, has been rising slowly, but they are still not widely used, and family planning information is not readily available.

Abortion, legal and free in Russia since 1920, is still the common form of birth control, as it was in the Soviet period. Although the rate has been declining in recent years, more than two million abortions are registered each year (not including unreported ones), and 10 percent of women who undergo the procedure are left sterile. According to U.S. demographer Murray Feshbach, two of every three pregnancies in Russia end in abortion, and women, on average, have six to eight abortions during their lifetime; at least 80 percent of all women have a pathology (abnormality) during pregnancy; and only 30 percent of all children are born healthy.[70]

A few more facts will help to describe the status of women in Russia. One of every two marriages ends in divorce, and the number of single mothers and single women continues to rise. Nearly one-third of all babies born in Russia in the year 2000 were born to unwed mothers, double the percentage of a decade earlier, and 40 percent of those babies were born to teenagers.[71]

Promiscuity is common but exists side by side with extreme modesty. While glasnost lowered official barriers to nudity and sexually explicit scenes in films, television, and theater, most Russians of the middle and older generations feel uncomfortable with those new liberties, and sex is not a subject for public discussion. Prudery also prevails. A woman will never ask a man for directions to the ladies' room; the man would be even more embarrassed than the woman.

Feminism, like many other movements originating in the West, has been late in reaching Russia. Grassroots women's groups are springing up around the country, but feminism is not yet a mass movement. The equality that Russian women want differs from that of Western women. Russian women see themselves as far more traditional in their dealings with men and their views on domestic life. In dress and style, for example, they prefer glamor to comfort, femininity to practicality.

Russian women are duly recognized, however, on one day of the year, Women's Day, a Russian version of Valentine's Day.[72] In communist years the festival was used to emphasize the equality of sexes lacking in the capitalist West, but it remains popular today. On March 8, women are showered with gifts from their loved ones. Food stores are jammed with shoppers seeking delicacies for the traditional meal at home. Jewelry and gift shops stay open late, and red roses and chocolates are in high demand as Russian men make amends for how they treat their women the rest of the year.

To cope with their hardships, women depend on and support each other to a remarkable degree. Through networks of trusted and lifelong friends, they help one another with the daily hassles of life and provide moral support in times of crisis.

How does all this affect Western women traveling to Russia on business? One veteran of many such visits warns that Russian men will turn on the charm, but their basic attitude toward a female visitor will be patronizing. Her professional qualifications will be regarded initially with some skepticism, and the Western woman will have to prove herself before she will be taken seriously. But as one Russian advised, "We judge women as we judge everyone else, according to their poise, personal strength of character, and whether they demonstrate an air of authority." Indeed, Western women, as well as men, will be judged by their professional expertise, seriousness of purpose, cultural level, and knowledge of Russia and its history.

Another Western woman scholar with long experience in Russia suggests a few stratagems that may help women to gain recognition from Russian professional contacts. An expensive-looking business card (bilingual preferred) and an advanced degree or title will attract attention. Namedropping will likewise impress, as will letters sent in advance by prominent persons vouching for the visitor.

Unemployment is much higher for women, and many of them look for marriage abroad. Others, mostly young women, turn to prostitution; literally thousands of them can be found on the main streets and in hotels, clubs,

and casinos in Moscow and St. Petersburg. Others are lured abroad by promises of employment but then find themselves prisoners in foreign bordellos.

Sex may also play a role in Russian contacts with Westerners. Foreign
visitors, male as well as female, may find that they are objects of considerable interest from the opposite sex. Before becoming romantically involved,
however, they should understand that it may be their passport rather than
their person that is the principal attraction. According to a Russian joke, a
foreigner is not just a future spouse but also a means of transportation (from
Russia).

Americans considering marriage to a Russian should heed the advice of
American author Lynn Visson:

> While Americans are attracted by the emotional intensity, close relation-
> ships, and cultural richness of Russian life, Russians are captivated by
> free and easy Americans and the wide range of opportunities held out by
> the United States. Where Russian women look for strong, caring, and
> sober American husbands, American women seek romantic, passionate
> Russian spouses. And while American men are attracted to feminine,
> "old-fashioned" Russian women, Russians are intrigued by the energetic
> and independent American working wives. . . . For better or worse, in
> the years to come, more and more Russians and Americans are likely to
> become involved in the most exciting and permanent of bilateral
> exchanges—marriage. The risks are great, and the losses can be enormous.
> So can the rewards.[73]

MESSIANISM

The Occident disappears, everything collapses, everything totters in a general
conflagration: the Europe of Charlemagne and the Europe of the treaties of
1815, the papacy of Rome and all the kingdoms of the West, Catholicism and
Protestantism, faith long lost and reason reduced to absurdity. Order becomes
henceforth impossible, freedom becomes henceforth impossible, and Occiden-
tal civilization commits suicide on top of all the ruins accumulated by it. . . .
And when we see rise above this immense wreck this even more immense East-
ern Empire like the Ark of the Covenant, who could doubt its mission. . . .

—Fyodor Tyutchev, *The Rock of Refuge*

Fyodor Tyutchev, a Russian diplomat and poet, wrote those words in 1848
in response to the liberal revolutions sweeping Western Europe in that year.
He saw Western civilization as disintegrating while Russian civilization,
morally and spiritually superior, was rising.

Messianism is still alive in Russia today, particularly among intellectuals, on the left as well as the right, who share a belief and pride in Russia as a great power with a special mission in the world. Economist Mikhail F. Antonov, for example, in an interview with *The New York Times Magazine,* showed that Tyutchev's belief in Russia's messianic mission and superiority was still very much alive.

"Let other countries surpass us in the technology of computer production," said Antonov, "but only we can provide an answer to the question: Why? For whose sake? We are the only legitimate heirs to the great, spiritual Russian culture. The saving of the world will come from Soviet Russia."[74]

Tyutchev and Antonov epitomize Russian thinkers, past and present, who seek to excuse her material backwardness by acclaiming her correctness of cause, spiritual superiority, and messianic mission.

"The notion of 'Holy Russia' runs deep," writes Serge Schmemann of *The New York Times,* "of a people lacking the German's industriousness or the American's entrepreneurship, but endowed with unique spirituality and mission."[75]

A similar view was espoused by a contemporary Russian philosopher when I asked him about Russia's role in the world. "Russia is European on the surface," he told me," but deep inside it is Asian, and our link between Europe and Asia is the Russian soul. Russia's mission is to unite Europe and Asia."

Such messianic missions are not unknown to Americans, who at times have also believed that they have something special to bring to the less fortunate—Christianity to heathens, democracy to dictatorships, and the free market to state-run economies. In his State of the Union message of 1991, President George H. W. Bush also delivered a message of messianism:

> For two centuries, America has served the world as an inspiring example of freedom and democracy. For generations, America has led the struggle to preserve and extend the blessings of liberty. And today, in a rapidly changing world, American leadership is indispensable. . . . But we also know why the hopes of humanity turn to us. We are Americans: we have a unique responsibility to do the hard work of freedom.[76]

A similar note was struck 14 years later by his son, President George W. Bush, in his State of the Union address on February 2, 2005:

> The attack on freedom in our world has reaffirmed our confidence in freedom's power to change the world. We are all part of a great venture:

to extend the promise of freedom in our country, to renew the values that sustain our liberty, and to spread the peace that freedom brings.[77]

Americans who believe in their own mission should be sensitive to Russian messianism and fears for the future. Without great-power status, Russians fear that other countries will no longer give them the respect they are due and Russia will lose its influence in the world.

Along with messianism, there is also a Russian tendency to blame others for their misfortunes, which has a certain logic. If Russians are indeed the chosen people and have a monopoly on truth, then others must be the cause of their misfortunes.

Freemasons and Jews, among others, have often been blamed in the past for Russia's troubles. And with nationalism resurgent, Jews are again being blamed, this time for Russia's ills. Indeed, as Russia goes through wrenching economic and social changes, anti-Semitic incidents have become more frequent among elected political leaders as well as the public at large. However, there is no official discrimination against Jews, and a poll in November 2000 by the late Yuri Levada, the respected Russian pollster, suggested that only 12 percent of the population had expressed openly anti-Semitic attitudes, which he said was about the same amount as in Europe.[78] Levada also believed that rabid anti-Semites comprise only about 3 to 4 percent of Russia's population.[79] In a gesture of support for Russia's Jews, in September 2000 then President Putin participated in the dedication of a new seven-story, mammoth Jewish community center in Moscow, and visited the site of a Moscow synagogue that had suffered a serious fire in 1993 and bomb attacks in 1996 and 1998.[80] In another symbolic gesture, Putin lit a national menorah, the traditional Jewish candelabra, to mark the beginning of the holiday of Hanukah in 2000. And in 2007, a rabbi was appointed as a chaplain in the Russian army, the first one since the Bolshevik revolution of 1917.

REBELLION AND REVOLT

God defend you from the sight of a Russian rebellion in all its ruthless stupidity.

—Aleksandr Pushkin, *The Captain's Daughter*

The Russians' patience sometimes wears thin and they rebel. History is replete with rebellions of serfs against masters, peasants against gentry, cossacks against lords, nobles against princes, and communists against commissars—

usually with mindless destruction and wanton cruelty. There is also a record of revolt from within—palace revolutions—in the time of general secretaries and presidents as well as tsars, as Mikhail Gorbachev learned in August 1991 when a junta attempted to seize power in Moscow, and as Boris Yeltsin learned in 1993 when a similar attempt was made by hard-liners in the Russian parliament.

Conspiracies, coups, insurrections, ethnic warfare, and national independence movements all reflect the instabilities and inequities of Russian society and its resistance to change. When peaceful evolution is not viable, revolution becomes inevitable.

Russians have long been seen as submissive to authority, politically passive, and unswerving in policy. But when the breaking point is reached, the submissive citizen spurns authority, the docile worker strikes, the passive person becomes politically active, and rigid policies are reversed almost overnight.

Such a point was reached in the late 1980s when the Soviet Union experienced food shortages, crippling strikes, a deteriorating economy, nationality unrest, ethnic warfare, movements for sovereignty or independence by the republics, inept government responses to the Chernobyl nuclear disaster and Armenian earthquake, and revelations of widespread environmental devastation.

In reaction to these events, voters of the Russian Federation rebelled in June 1991. Given a choice, they rejected the candidates of communism and chose as their president Boris Yeltsin and his program of decentralization, democracy, and economic reform. Yeltsin thus became the first freely elected leader in Russian history.

In August 1991, Russians rebelled again, taking to the streets of Moscow in a massive protest that helped bring down the old guard junta that had attempted to seize power. And in December 1995, disillusioned with reform, corruption, and a deep decline in their standard of living, Russians repudiated the Yeltsin administration by electing a parliament that was deeply divided between opponents and supporters of democratic and economic reforms, and between Westernizers and Slavophiles.

WESTERNIZERS AND SLAVOPHILES

To Russia, in its hunger for civilization, the West seemed "the land of miracles. . . ."

—Thomas Masaryk, *The Spirit of Russia*

Russia's love-hate relationship with the West has given rise to two schools of thought—Westernizers and Slavophiles. Both can be regarded as Russian patriots, although they have held opposing views on Russia's position in the world.

Westernizers, recognizing Russia's backwardness, sought to borrow from the West in order to modernize. They saw Russia as a political entity that would benefit from Western enlightenment, rationalism, rule of law, technology, manufacturing, and the growth of a middle class. Among the Westernizers were political reformers, liberals, and socialists.

Slavophiles also sought to borrow from the West, but they were determined to protect and preserve Russia's unique cultural values and traditions. They rejected individualism and regarded the Church, rather than the state, as Russia's leading historical and moral force. Admirers of agricultural life, they were critical of urban development and industrialization. Slavophiles, moreover, sought to preserve the mir in order to prevent the growth of a Russian proletariat. They opposed socialism as alien to Russia and preferred Russian mysticism to Western rationalism. Among the Slavophiles were philosophical conservatives, nationalists, and the Church.

The controversy between Westernizers and Slavophiles has appeared in many forms in Russian history. As Hugh Seton-Watson pointed out, it divided Russian socialism between Marxists and Populists, Russian Marxists between Mensheviks and Bolsheviks, and Bolsheviks between opponents and followers of Stalin.[81] The controversy has been between those who believed in Europe and those who believed in Russia.

In our time, the conflict continues between supporters and opponents of reform, modernizers and traditionalists, internationalists and nationalists. Today's conservative Russians who seek to preserve Russia's faith and harmony are ideological descendants of the Slavophiles. For them, the moral basis of society takes priority over individual rights and material progress, a view held today by many Russians, noncommunist as well as communist. As Aleksandr Solzhenitsyn said from his self-imposed seclusion in Vermont, 15 years after his forced exile from the Soviet Union:

> There is technical progress [in the West], but this is not the same thing as the progress of humanity as such. . . . In Western civilization—which used to be called Western-Christian, but now might better be called Western-Pagan—along with the development of intellectual life and science there has been a loss of the serious moral basis of society. During these 300 years of Western civilization, there has been a sweeping away of duties and

an expansion of rights . . . the only thing we have been developing is rights, rights, rights, at the expense of duty.[82]

That school of thought, epitomized by Solzhenitsyn, has given Russia a superiority complex toward the West in things ethereal and an inferiority complex in matters material. The West is seen as spiritually impoverished and decadent, and Russia as morally rich and virtuous.

In the current environment of rapid change, Russian governments have made repeated appeals for a renewal of moral values and the search for a new "Russian idea" to embody them. Vladimir Putin, as president, repeatedly stated that Russia's renewal depends not only on economic success or correct state policies but on a revival of moral values and national spirit, and he has called for a new "Russian idea" that emphasizes patriotism, social protections, a strong state, and great-power status. As Georgi Poltavchenko, one of Putin's KGB lieutenants from St. Petersburg, explained:

> The country must have a Russian ideology! Since the Lord ordained our special path, we must also have our own ideology. The most important thing is to primarily instill patriotism and love for the motherland. Then it is the business and right of each person to have their own political views, but you must be a patriot of your own state.[83]

That idea presumes a unique Russian way, with values superior to those of the materialist, individualistic, and decadent West, an idea that has also been embraced by various nationalist and communist political parties.

Among those taking up the "Russian idea" are the neo-Eurasianists, who trace their roots to a movement that originated among Russian exiles in Western Europe in the early 1920s. One of the early Eurasian spokesmen, economic geographer Pyotr Savitsky, wrote in 1925:

> The idea of a Europe that combines Western and Eastern Europe is absurd. [Eurasia] is a world apart, distinct from the countries situated on the West and on those situated on the South and the South-East. Russia occupies the greatest part of the Eurasian landmass; it is not divided between two continents but forms a third, independent geographic entity.[84]

Today's Eurasianists also reject the West and see Russia's future in the East. They advocate a union of the three Slavic peoples—Russians, Belarusians, and Ukrainians—and a federation of the Slavic peoples with their Turkic neighbors to the south and east in a political union that looks strikingly similar to the former Soviet Union—and with the Russians in charge. Among the more prominent Eurasianists are Gennadi Zyuganov, leader of the Russian Communist Party, and Vladimir Zhirinovsky, the ultranationalist leader of the so-called Liberal Democratic Party. In the March 2000 presidential election, Zyuganov received 29.2 percent of the vote and Zhirinosvky 2.7 percent, a far cry from the 1993 parliamentary elections when Zhirinosvky's party surprisingly won almost one-fourth of the vote.

Four years later, however, Putin swept the election for president with 71.3 percent of the vote, while the runner-up, Nikolai Kharitonov, had only 13.7 percent, and Zyuganov and Zhirinovsky did not run. And in the March 2008 election for president, Dmitri Medvedev received 70.28 percent of the vote, Zyuganov 17.72 percent, and Zhirinovsky 9.34 percent.

FOUR

State and Society

With the mind alone Russia cannot be understood,
No ordinary yardstick spans her greatness;
She stands alone, unique—
In Russia one can only believe.

—Fyodor Tyutchev

THE RUSSIAN HERITAGE

If men could foresee the future, they would still behave as they do now.

—Russian proverb

"I have seen the future and it works," wrote an American writer after visiting Russia in 1919. That euphoric vision, attributed to journalist and author Lincoln Steffens, we now know was twice mistaken. The Soviet state did not portend the future, and Soviet society did not work.

To be sure, state and society were turned upside down by the Great October Revolution—as communists call the Bolshevik seizure of power in 1917. The small, French-speaking elite that had ruled Russia was removed from power by confiscation of land and property, exile, or outright murder. In theory, the new ruling class was to be composed of workers and peasants, represented by local *sovieti* (councils) and guided by the Communist Party.

In practice, however, after Stalin had eliminated his rivals, one autocracy was replaced by another.

Building on the utopian dreams of generations of Russian thinkers, the Bolsheviks planned to create a new state—and a new "Soviet person"—that would correct all of old Russia's inequities. By applying the principles of what they called "scientific socialism"—a Western import—they would establish the new order by nationalizing production, instituting central planning, abolishing private property, and redistributing wealth according to the Marxist maxim as modified by the Soviets: "From each according to his capacities, to each according to his work." And all this was to be accomplished under the direction of the Communist Party, which, as the Soviet Constitution put it, would be "the leading and guiding force of Soviet society and the nucleus of its political system."

The Bolsheviks, however, found themselves heirs to many relics of tsarist Russia—a vast multinational empire dominated by Russians, governed from its center, and ruled by coercion rather than law; a state-imposed ideology that set standards for citizen behavior; a bureaucracy that was arrogant, corrupt, and incompetent; the priority of the community over the individual; a pervasive censorship; suspicion of dissidents and others who thought differently; and a ubiquitous secret police to enforce the state's will.

Americans who rail against the intrusions of the U.S. government in their lives should try to imagine a state and society that is run like a huge corporation without competitors, a monopoly controlled and managed by insiders. In this corporation, individual rights are subordinated to the greater communal good, as seen by the board of directors, whose decisions are final.

The United States also had a revolution, but it did not turn the social structure upside down. Its population was homogeneous, mostly of English origin at the time of the revolution, numbering only two million, and living in relative proximity along the Atlantic coast. The system of governance, based on English common law, economic liberalism, and individual rights, did portend the future, and it worked. America's models were England and Western enlightenment. The models for Russia were Byzantium and Mongol rule.

Today's Russia, neither European nor Asian, has also inherited the problems of the past. In many ways it is a developed country, with heavy industry, high technology, world-class science, an educated populace, formidable military strength, and nuclear power. In other ways it is a developing country, with poverty, inefficiency, low productivity, poor public health, a primitive

58

infrastructure, and disregard for the rule of law. It is that third-world Russia that reformers are attempting to coax into the modern world.

Experts, both Russian and Western, are divided on the prospects for reform. But whatever the results, they can be expected to reflect the values and views that are deeply rooted in the Russian past. Much as the Soviet Union retained many key elements of the Russian past, so too will the new Russia, in many ways, resemble the old. As an economist in Prague has written, "Top-down imposition of socialism ended in failure. Let's wait and see how top-down imposition of capitalism will end."[85]

STATISM

Who serves the Tsar cannot serve the people.

—Russian proverb

Russians have a deep and abiding suspicion of government. Public opinion polls show that the vast majority of Russians are convinced that most of their leaders hold public office only for personal gain and do not care about the concerns of the common person. This estrangement from government is very high and is based, in part, on past experience.

In the past, Russian governments have served rulers rather than the ruled, so why should the populace believe things will be different now? Until Russia's free elections of 1991, democratic governance was experienced only once, in 1917, during the brief period between the democratic February revolution and the Bolshevik October Revolution. With those exceptions, authoritarianism has been the rule in Russian governance.

"There is little in the country's past," writes Robert G. Kaiser, "that has prepared it to become a modern, tolerant, and efficient democracy. Russians have no real experience with independent civic institutions, checks and balances, or even the restrained use of power. Russian citizens have been estranged from the state for many centuries. . . ."[86]

For centuries, Russia was an absolute monarchy, ruled as a paramilitary garrison state to guard against threats both internal and external. As George Vernadsky, Yale University's distinguished professor of Russian history, described it: "In the Tsardom of Moscow of the sixteenth and seventeenth centuries we find an entirely new concept of society and its relation to the state. All the classes of the nation, from top to bottom, except the slaves, were bound to the service of the state . . ."[87] That state, moreover, was ruled by hereditary tsars who held absolute power, issuing decrees that had the force of law. The Russian *ukaz* (decree) has come into English as *ukase*, a decree having force of law. In the 1990s, Boris Yeltsin also ruled by decree, as tsars and commissars had done before him; Vladimir Putin, Yeltsin's successor, also had extraordinary powers, even under the Constitution of 1993. As Yuri Afanasyev, a leading reformer in the 1980s, put it:

> It was characteristic of Russia to have the people at the "bottom" harshly subordinated to the people at the "top," and for people generally to be subordinated to the state; such relations were formed back in the twelfth century. The eternal oppression in Russia created a reaction against it of intolerance, aggression, and hostility; and it is this oppression and the reaction to it that create cruelty and mass violence.[88]

Russia's rulers, perceiving domestic unrest and political dissent as threats to their ability to govern a vast empire, have not hesitated to use force to maintain their authority. They saw Russia surrounded by hostile or unstable powers, and they took advantage of any weakness or instability along their state's periphery to secure its borders and extend its territorial reach.

With power concentrated at the center, the influence of the state on Russian society has been pervasive. In old Russia, the largest landholders were the crown, the church, and the aristocracy. Many sectors of the economy were controlled or subsidized by the state. For both rulers and the ruled, service to the state was the primary duty.

In the Soviet era, the state played an even larger role. Moscow's heavy hand was found in the economy, culture, education, the media, religion, and citizens' private lives—planning, directing, instructing, and stifling initiative in the process. Big Brother—or rather Big Daddy, in a paternalistic society— was everywhere. And Putin, although supposedly committed to a free market, restored state direction over the economy.

Russians, moreover, have often idolized their leaders. The tsar was seen as the *tsar-batyushka* (tsar-father). Stalin was similarly adored as a father figure. And Putin, unknown prior to being named by Yeltsin as his successor, has regularly received approval ratings of more than 70 percent, which is almost identical with the vote Medvedev, a relative unknown, received in his 2008 election as president.

Commenting on Russian governance, George F. Kennan wrote:

> Forms of government and the habits of governments tend over the long run to reflect the understandings and expectations of their peoples. The

Russian people . . . have never known democracy as we understand it. They have experienced next to nothing of the centuries-long development of the discipline of self-government out of which our own political culture has evolved.[89]

The result has been a submissive citizenry, accustomed to—indeed expecting—direction from above, being told what to do and what to think. "It is difficult for us to make decisions," a Russian psychologist told me. "We are so used to being told what to do that we cannot take the initiative and decide for ourselves." Such an attitude helps to explain the reluctance of individual Russians to become involved in issues that they believe are the responsibility of government and where the role of the individual citizen seems insignificant.

Another centuries-old tradition is a state-sanctioned ideology that serves as a moral guide, determining what is right and wrong. In the tsarist era, the ideology was Russian Orthodoxy, the state religion. In the Soviet period, the Communist Party imposed its own standards of cultural, moral, and political behavior. Today, Russia is searching for a new ideology—a "Russian idea" to serve as a moral guide.

The contrasts between Russia and the United States are again apparent. In the latter, state power has been limited and diffused, both within the federal government and between federal and state authorities. Free elections and a multiparty system have ensured representation of the popular will. A government role in culture and the media has been eschewed. Church and state have been separate and the rights of religious minorities protected. The development of moral and cultural values has been left to private institutions independent of government—the churches, the media, universities, and that typically American institution, the private voluntary organization. An economy based on private property and the free market, although at times assisted and regulated by the government, has remained free from state control. It's not perfect, but as Winston Churchill once put it, ". . . democracy is the worst form of government except all the others that have been tried."

THE BUREAUCRACY

More than in any other country, officials in Russia considered themselves a superior species, appointed to drive the herds of human cattle. Obedience and patience were required of the cattle, willingness to wait for hours and days for a decision, and acceptance of the decision when given.

—Hugh Seton-Watson, *The Decline of Imperial Russia*

In his description of Russian officials, the British historian Hugh Seton-Watson was writing about nineteenth-century Russia. His words, however, would be equally valid for the Russia of our time, where the tradition of an omnipotent, obstinate, and obstructionist bureaucracy still exists. Foreign visitors who interact with Russians will need to understand this bureaucracy and learn how to deal with it.

A diplomatic colleague of mine who had previously served in Iran and Syria told me that after his posting to Moscow he felt very much at home. As in the Middle East, he explained, papers went from desk to desk in the bureaucracy, responsibility was diluted, and decisions were referred to higher-ups. (He might have added that such behavior is not limited to Russia and the Middle East but is also found in most developing countries.)

Before proceeding with joint endeavors, the approval of all the government agencies involved will be needed, which is easier said than done. Doing business in Russia, explained John Blaney, a former economics counselor at the American Embassy in Moscow, is "almost like a three-dimensional chess game, where each level has different rules and different pieces, and every once in a while, on any level, all the rules change."[90]

Some Russian officials, to be sure, are creative, decisive, and motivated and could easily hold their own in London's "City" or New York's Wall Street. They are exceptions, however, and stand out among the others. Most bureaucrats whom foreigners will meet—"dead souls" they have been called in Russian—prefer to follow established practice rather than show initiative and risk errors that might put their careers at risk. Under the communists, initiative was not rewarded, and many of today's high officials are holdovers from the communist past.

The result is rigidity, incompetence, sloth, conservatism, and a tendency to avoid responsibility by passing the buck to higher-ups. Supervisory officials, moreover, are responsible for the errors of their underlings and can be severely disciplined when mistakes are made. What to do?

As one veteran Russian interpreter advised me, "Foreigners should understand that many Russian officials they will do business with are incompetent and hold their jobs only because of nepotism, friendships, or party membership. Visitors should try in advance to get the names of competent officials and seek them out." That can be done with a little homework—

contacting colleagues who have previously negotiated with Russian official-dom and learned which officials to seek out and which to avoid.

At higher levels of the bureaucracy during the communist era was the *nomenklatura,* the lifelong, tenured positions filled by Communist Party appointees on the basis of political reliability. Wielding unchallenged power, the nomenklatura had a vested interest in maintaining the status quo and was positioned to block or slow down change. That elite had its own lifestyle—better housing, access to special "closed stores" and upscale vacation resorts, superior medical care, and the highest award for loyalty, foreign travel. With the collapse of communism the nomenklatura was expected to disappear, but like many other elements of Russian society it has reappeared with many of the same perks.

Today's nomenklatura, many of them holdovers from the Soviet era, also has free housing, free medical care in the best clinics and hospitals, vacations at resorts formerly reserved for the Soviet elite, cars, weekend dachas, and many other privileges. But instead of stealing from the state under cover, they now do it openly.

Among today's privileged are also the privatizers, the "new rich," as well as the government officials whose cooperation they buy with bribes. The perks of this moneyed class are also little different from those of the old nomenklatura—luxury goods, better housing, quality medical care, superior schooling for their children, foreign travel and possession of wealth outside Russia, and freedom from constraints of the law.

Bureaucrats today still issue licenses and permits, control municipal housing and land transfers for commercial and other uses, set export quotas for various commodities, and give approvals for new businesses. Opportunities for corruption are everywhere, and the old Russian tradition of stealing from the state continues. Some refer to the new Russia today as a "kleptocracy."

How should you deal with these officials whose approval will be needed for joint endeavors? First, start discussions as high in the chain of command as possible. Decisions on foreign proposals are rarely made at the working level but are usually referred to more senior officials. The higher you start, the closer you will be to the person who makes the decisions. Indeed, when petitioners are able to state their case directly to an official with authority, decisions are made more promptly, if not immediately. But that presents another challenge—to determine who has the authority and who decides.

Prepare the groundwork by presenting in advance a paper outlining your proposal. That will give the bureaucracy time to study the offer, check it out with higher officials, and give a more authoritative response. Such a paper will also help to ensure that the proposal is accurately presented as it works its way up through the bureaucracy. To conform with the Russian approach (the concept first and then the details), begin the paper with a general introduction—the background, history, and even philosophy behind the proposal—before proceeding to the particulars.

An initial nyet should not be accepted as a definitive response. Russians can change positions when they know more about a proposal and are persuaded that it is in their interest. Keep talking. Negotiations may be lengthy and decisions slow in coming (see Chapter 6, "Negotiating with Russians"). Everything takes longer in Russia and requires patience and perseverance.

Germans, who have been doing business with Russia for centuries, have learned from experience. "Many American businessmen," says one German banker, "come to Moscow and leave three weeks later completely frustrated. German businessmen are willing to stay six months to make a deal."[91]

One reason why things take longer is that Russians feel more comfortable with persons they have known for some time. The familiar face is welcome, and repeated visits to Russia may be necessary before confidence and trust are built.

Gift giving is an old Eastern custom. In Slavic lands visitors have been traditionally welcomed with gifts of bread and salt, the staples of life, as the U.S. astronauts were when they docked with the Russian space station *Mir* in June 1995. (The Americans brought flowers and chocolates.)

The tradition of exchanging gifts continues, but the staples of life have changed. Bribes are illegal, of course, but between a gift and a bribe there is a narrow line that may be difficult to discern. In any event, the gift of a DVD player, computer, or stereo system will grease the wheels—as well as the palms—of the bureaucracy. Less costly items will also be appreciated—new movie DVDs, popular music CDs, electronic gadgets, Scotch whiskey, and almost anything Western. Women will be grateful for perfume, cosmetics, costume jewelry, chocolates, and fancy soaps. Good tea is always appreciated, but in bulk rather than tea bags.

Bring a bag of souvenirs, especially those with a university, company, or city logo. Russians are avid collectors of souvenir pins. And in a nation of bibliophiles, books are treasured. Particularly welcome are recent publications by well-known authors, but almost anything new in English will do.

Breaking bread breaks barriers. Russians welcome invitations to lunch or dinner where business can be conducted informally and where they will not be speaking "on the record." The working breakfast, however, which is alien to Russian culture, is only slowly coming into vogue. More common is the "*biznes* lunch" between 1:00 P.M. and 3:00 P.M. Visitors from abroad may be invited to Russian homes now that the risk of association with foreigners is gone. Favors are appreciated and will be reciprocated.

The greatest favor would be a much-prized invitation to visit a foreign country, with costs covered by the host. Russians have an enormous interest in foreign travel, but in the Soviet period travel was limited to a favored few. Now it is much easier to obtain a Russian passport and exit visa, and more than 18 million Russians traveled abroad in 2007.

Many visitors wonder why they seldom see papers on desks in the offices where they are received. This is because many of the higher officials have two offices—one for work and another for receiving visitors.

CRIME AND CORRUPTION

It's easy to steal when seven others are stealing.

—Russian proverb

As in many Eastern countries, what counts is not what you know but whom you know, and often whom you pay off. *Blat* (influence or pull) is a way of life in Russia, along with its first cousin, nepotism. Officials have long been accustomed to using their positions to help themselves, their families, and friends. But today, for most Russians, corruption is a way of life. A discreet gift will bring favorable treatment in government offices. Knowing the right person can mean receiving an apartment or gaining admission to a preferred school or university. Bribery can get a young man an exemption from military service.

Transparency International, the Berlin-based nonprofit, nonpartisan organization founded to curb corruption in international transactions, ranked Russia at a new low of 143 out of 179 countries in its annual Corruptions Perception Index for 2007, with Russia rank-listed between Indonesia and Togo. (The bottom three countries were Iraq, Myanmar, and Somalia; the top-rated countries were Denmark, Finland, New Zealand, Singapore, and Sweden. The United Kingdom occupied 12th place, and the United States 20th.)[92]

Everything in Russia is for sale at the right price. Tax breaks are sold for foreign currency, timber rights are given in exchange for Western cars, criminal investigations are halted for payoffs, federal funds are deposited in certain banks in exchange for bribes, property leases are extended for cash, and police protection is sold for bribes. Managers loot their firms by not paying bills and sending their capital abroad. The list goes on and on.

"Bribes used to be given in envelopes" said one Russian. "Now they are given in cartons," a reference not only to inflation but to the increase in the amount of the bribes. One American contractor who works in Russia describes the bribes he must pay there as "solicited gratuities, an accepted cost of doing business."

Bribery and embezzlement were common in old Russia, as Nikolai Gogol told us in his comic classic, *The Inspector General,* but they were also common in the Soviet era, although they were seldom brought to light and definitely were not the subject of literature. Under glasnost, however, after Gorbachev assumed power in 1985, an epidemic of corruption in high places was exposed and offenders were brought to trial.

Most disconcerting to Russians is that the illicit behavior long practiced by officials has now spread throughout the population and has become a way of life. Traffic police take bribes from motorists for minor infractions; teachers are paid to give students good grades; professors sell admission to top universities; and doctors in state-run hospitals demand payment for supposedly free care before treating patients. Almost anything can be "bought" with a payoff—to officials high as well as low.

Paying taxes is a new civic responsibility for Russians, and it is a responsibility for which the past years of a centrally planned economy have not prepared them. Consequently, tax collection has been a problem for every Russian government since 1991. As French economist Yves Gisse explains:

> A population which has been accustomed to receive free public services and other state support and not to pay new income taxes nor indirect taxes, will have difficulties to establish a strong tax administration system responsible for collecting personal and corporate taxes at the country level. There again, it is a matter of a new cultural adaptation to economic change.[93]

Corruption has also become a way of doing business in the private sector. The key players are government officials who issue licenses for new businesses and control natural resources; traders and financiers who can move money and goods around; and protection racketeers who are hired to ensure that business deals are honored. Corruption has also become a means of survival for underpaid officials who are seeking to support their families on meager salaries.

Crime has also been rising sharply in Russia, with major increases reported for consumer cheating, evasion of customs duties, drug trafficking, theft of arms and munitions, and apartment robberies. The increased crime is troubling to Russians, and public opinion polls show that they place it high on their list of greatest grievances. Russians assume that everything and everyone has been bought, and as a consequence they do not trust anyone outside their immediate circle of family and friends. Their prime motivation appears to be how to protect and benefit their own family in these trying times.

Also troubling are the machinations of the mafia.

THE MAFIA

Organized crime has supplanted many of the functions of the state. A coalition of organized crime and former Party elites provides the ruling elites of many regions of Russia and many other CIS states. Organized crime provides many of the services that citizens expect from their state—protection of commercial businesses, employment for citizens, mediation in disputes. Private security, often run by organized crime, is replacing state law enforcement.

—Louise I. Shelley, *Demokratizatsiya*

Mafia is the term used by Russians to describe the vast network of gangsters and racketeers who are said to control much of the Russian economy, including private businesses, banks, and markets, and who are responsible for much of the violence that permeates society. Newcomers to Russia should be aware, though, that Russians apply the term *mafia* indiscriminately, using it also to describe legitimate entrepreneurs and others who have achieved financial success in the new Russia.

Accustomed as Americans may be to violence, it is difficult for them to imagine the level in Russia. The homicide rate is three times that of the United States, but while in the U.S. most victims are from lower income groups, in Russia victims are usually business and higher income people. Contract killings mostly "hit" mid-level officials in the oil and gas, metals, and banking sectors. Foreign business people and Russian highflyers have not generally been targeted, but judges are intimidated, and prosecutors and investigative journalists have been assassinated. Journalists have been particularly vulnerable, and since the Soviet Union broke up, more than 80 have been assassinated in connection with their work.[94]

Russia and the world were shocked when Duma Deputy Galina Starovoytova was gunned down in St. Petersburg in 1998. More recent killings that have attracted worldwide attention include the shooting of journalist and human rights activist Anna Politkovskaya, widely known for her fierce opposition to the Chechen war and the Putin administration, who was gunned down in her Moscow apartment building in 2006, and the mysterious death of former KGB lieutenant-colonel Alexander Litvinenko, who died of radiation poisoning in 2006 in London, where he had been living under political asylum. The mafia consists of regionally or market-based criminal groups, distinct from each other but linked by cooperative arrangements. They began after the breakup of the Soviet Union by controlling illegal activities—gambling, prostitution, stolen cars, and narcotics—and have since branched out and spread their influence in virtually all aspects of Russian private life; they have even reached abroad to Western Europe, the United States, and Israel. The Russian mafia extorts money—and in some cases demands a share in ownership—from small privately owned businesses as well as banks, large businesses, and even some of the new Western-built hotels frequented by foreign visitors. One of the mafia's main activities is to provide the protection that private property owners require but are unable to obtain from the legitimate authorities. Through its international contacts, the mafia is also engaged in the illegal export of oil and other commodities, the smuggling of weapons and nuclear materials, the laundering of money, and the flight of much-needed capital abroad.

The Russian mafia's roots are not in Italy (whence comes the word *mafia*) but rather in the Soviet political system, which exercised power through criminality and violence. In this sense, the mafia has replaced the Communist Party by providing "order" in Russia. Indeed, the mafia is believed to be an alliance between criminals and former communists in the state bureaucracy, including the KGB, the source of many of its strong-arm henchmen.

Organized crime in Russia and the other states of the former Soviet Union inhibits the growth of democracy, corrupts domestic politics, discourages foreign investment and economic assistance, depletes natural resources, and deprives domestic economies of capital. Unless curbed, it will be a festering threat to Russia's future.

The most disturbing aspect of mafia activity in Russia, says Marshall Goldman, "is that a growing number of Russians have come to believe that this distorted form of mafia control is what a free market system means."[95]

THE KGB

I am giving away no secrets when I reveal that the new Russian intelligence service is pretty much the old K.G.B. in drag.

—John le Carré, "My New Friends in Russia"

One part of the Russian bureaucracy that works well is the successor organizations to the Committee on State Security (KGB) of the Soviet era. The new Foreign Intelligence Service (SVR) has inherited the foreign intelligence components of the KGB, while the Federal Security Service (FSB) is responsible for internal security. A third successor, the Main Guard Administration (GUO), has responsibility for the president's personal security and the security of the Kremlin and other government buildings. The acronyms have changed but they are all commonly known to Russians as the KGB—as they will be referred to in this book—and they do much of the same work. Indeed, their officers today still refer to themselves as *Chekists,* from *Cheka* (Extraordinary Committee Against Sabotage and Counter-Revolution), the name of the secret police organization founded in 1917 by Felix Dzerzhinsky, one of the original Bolsheviks.

KGB activities abroad are well known to Westerners through films and novels as well as news reports. Less known abroad are its domestic responsibilities embodied in legislation confirmed by Boris Yeltsin in April 1995. These include combating organized crime, creating enterprises as fronts for investigative work, controlling state secrets, operating its own prison system, and providing security for the armed forces and the federal government.[96]

The KGB's mandate is broad, and so are its activities. Indeed, it is said that it is difficult to do anything in business in Russia today without some arrangement with the KGB, especially since many of Putin's senior appointees are former KGB officers. As a Russian journalist describes it:

> The KGB was not just the Soviet Union's most powerful institution, but also was *and is* [emphasis added] a corporation with its own, quite specific organizational culture that is driven by notions of the imperial state and disrespect for individual lives, freedoms and liberties.[97]

Russia has had a secret police since the sixteenth century when Tsar Ivan the Terrible established his *Oprichnina* to root out political opposition. The name has changed over the centuries and the scope of its activities has expanded considerably, but its essential purpose has not changed. Russian rulers have continued to maintain a secret police to counter domestic opposition and enforce their will. In the twenty-first century, Russia's democratically elected leaders recognize that they too need a security agency.

The KGB was Stalin's personal instrument for carrying out his reign of terror. According to a former KGB officer, material in KGB archives has disclosed that eighteen million people were "repressed" from 1935 to 1945—about seven million of whom were shot. These figures, however, do not include deaths in prison and labor camps or by means of execution other than shooting. Many historians, Russian as well as Western, believe that deaths due to the terror were far greater, approaching even the more than twenty million Soviets citizens who died in World War II.[98]

Whatever the number, Stalin's abuses were extensive, and there is hardly a family that was not in some way a victim. Today, with the KGB no longer the feared instrument of the past, Russians will not hesitate to tell visitors what their family members experienced during the terror.

Many of the Russian officials serving abroad or at home in state agencies that work with foreigners are KGB officers, or they have been co-opted by the KGB to report on their foreign contacts. Foreigners working with Russians will likely encounter such personnel at some point, although they may not be aware of it.

Encounters with KGB officers need not be a cause of concern. KGB personnel who serve abroad are among Russia's best and brightest. Intelligence, like science, is where the talent goes. Members of the KGB's First Directorate (foreign intelligence) are often the sons of privileged members of the nomenklatura. They are also likely to be intelligent—as well as intelligence—officers who demonstrate flexibility, initiative, and confidence in dealing with foreigners. Moreover, those who have served abroad have the knowledge and experience of the West that most Russians do not have. Today, in addition to military and political intelligence, their priorities may also include economic and technological data, but they will also be collecting and reporting information on people they meet.

What is the KGB looking for? Of interest are personal foibles and weaknesses that might be used for blackmail at some future time—unusual lifestyles, addictions, sexual preferences, and financial difficulties. Foreign visitors to Russia are no longer routinely followed, but hotel rooms and telephones may still be bugged and mail monitored. Any suspicious activity can be expected to attract KGB interest. And the KGB has a long memory. Once an item goes into a person's dossier, it may lie dormant for many years, to surface only when an earlier indiscretion has been long forgotten and the individual in question has reached a position of importance.

A warm personal relationship with a Russian, however, can thwart even the KGB. A former American exchange student in Russia relates how he was assigned to share a dormitory room with a Russian student. Entering his room one day, the American found his roommate amorously involved with a female visitor. "Disappear," growled the Russian. The American quickly retreated but stationed himself outside the door and prevented others from entering the room until the liaison had been concluded. In appreciation, the Russian confessed that he had been assigned by the KGB to report on his roommate. "But since you are such a fine fellow," he added, "just stay in your room and study for a few nights, and I'll say in my report that you are a serious scholar and not a CIA spy."

One final word of caution. Visitors to Russia should not say anything in public—or in a place where it might be overheard—that could get a Russian citizen in trouble with the authorities. Never mention to others the names of friends whose actions or views might make difficulties for them. When Russians trust someone, they will open up and tell everything, but they will also expect that person to respect the confidence.

THE LAW

If all laws perished, the people would live in truth and justice.

—Russian proverb

In Mr. Putin's seven years as president, a Soviet-style cynicism about the law has returned, one in which justice, like diplomacy, is simply a series of political calculations laced with ulterior motives, as opposed to a dispassionate search for truth, fairness and accountability.

—Steven Lee Myers, *The New York Times*, May 27, 2007

When Richard Nixon named his cabinet after winning the presidential election of 1968, a prominent Russian law professor asked me why so many lawyers had been chosen by the new president. Lawyers in the Soviet Union did not have much prestige, and Russians were puzzled by the prominence of lawyers in U.S. public life.

Lawyers in the Soviet Union had little social status or political influence, little importance in the legal system, and were poorly paid. More important than training in the law was position in the Communist Party. With the exception of Gorbachev and Lenin, who both studied law, Soviet political leaders were usually engineers by training. Yeltsin's education and work experience, for example, was in construction engineering, and Putin, although he had studied law, made his career in the KGB. That has been changing in the new Russia as owners of private property have found that they now need lawyers. And Russian lawyers are pleased that Russia's new president, Dmitri Medvedev, is a former law professor.

In response to the Russian professor's question, I first cited the trite but true textbook response that the United States has a government of laws and not of men. I next discussed the significance of private property in U.S. law and the importance of the contract, both of which may require lawyers. My third explanation—more meaningful in the Russian context—concerned the concept of compromise, the foundation of democracy. I explained that in U.S. civil disputes, most lawyers settle their cases through negotiation and compromise, while in criminal law most charges are settled through plea bargaining—a compromise between lawyers for the prosecution and defense. The meaning was not lost on the professor because *kompromis* in Russian has a pejorative meaning and is considered a sign of weakness and a breach of faith.

More important than the law in Russian culture have been truth and justice. The search for social justice is a continuing theme in Russian literature, from Tolstoy to Solzhenitsyn. Russian writers, reflecting their quest for social justice and universal harmony, have regretted their country's failure to assuage suffering and eliminate inequities.

"Bolshevism," wrote Nikolai Berdiaev, "showed itself to be much more faithful to certain primordial Russian traditions, to the Russian search for universal social justice . . . and to the Russian method of government and control by coercion."[99] Berdiaev, a prominent religious philosopher, had a youthful flirtation with Marxism but later became a strong critic of Bolshevism. Expelled from the Soviet Union in 1922, he settled in Paris.

For Russians, the consensus of the community has been more important than the legalisms of the law. Not surprisingly, Russians discount the law's ability to provide the truth and justice they seek.

In the mir, the rule of law did not apply. Decisions were made by the village assembly based on what made sense at the time and appeared just and useful for the common good. Crime was not considered by peasants in the abstract, as Nicholas Vakar has noted. Stealing wood from the state or a landowner, for example, was against the law, but it was not considered by peasants to be a crime. However, stealing even the smallest object from a fellow villager or the commune would bring the culprit a severe beating, at the very least, or even mutilation or death. And the horse thief, as in the American West, was one of society's worst enemies. If caught, he was promptly tortured and lynched without trial. The same was true for arsonists in a land where thatched huts burned quickly and an entire village could be destroyed quickly by fire.[100]

In tsarist Russia, rule was by imperial decree, and the tsar's will was not subject to law. As Richard Wortman has written, "The tsarist state, ever insistent on the supremacy of the executive power, has held the judicial system in disdain, and this disdain was shared by the officialdom and the nobility."[101]

Soviet leaders continued the tradition of being above the law. In the 1960s, when they mounted a campaign against foreign-currency speculators, several suspects were arrested and, in accordance with the Soviet penal code, were sentenced to long terms of imprisonment. Public opinion, however, whipped up by press reports on the speculators' high lifestyles, demanded the death penalty.

Nikita Khrushchev, Party chief at the time, summoned the public prosecutor general and demanded the death sentence. When told that Soviet law did not permit execution for currency speculation, Khrushchev replied, "Who's the boss, we or the law? We are masters over the law; not the law over us—so we have to change the law. . . ." And a law was indeed passed that accorded the death penalty for speculating in large sums of foreign currency, the speculators were tried—some for a second time—sentenced to death, and executed.[102]

Russian and Western law have a common ancestry in Roman law. Indeed, in the year 1000, wrote U.S. legal scholar Harold J. Berman, the law of Kievan Rus was similar to that of Germanic Europe and Anglo-Saxon England. But the Franks had converted to Christianity in 486, and Kievan Rus not until 988, and that put Russia five hundred years behind the West in the development of its legal system.[103]

Differences between Russian and Western law derive from Byzantium and Russian Orthodoxy. In Byzantium, the emperor had absolute authority over justice, making and unmaking laws, legislating on religious as well as civil matters, and acting as supreme judge of the land. Moreover, in Byzantium church and state were one, and the emperor was presumed to have the obligation to monitor the morals of his people. Russian law, accordingly, has been more intrusive in personal lives. The Orthodox

Church and Russian law have also emphasized community and a common sense of brotherhood and togetherness. This, said Berman, has given Russian law

> a strong tradition of collective social consciousness which relies for its motivation less on reason than on common faith and common worship, and which finds expression less in legal formality and "due process" than in more spontaneous and more impulsive responses.[104]

Moreover, added Berman, there is a Russian belief that large areas of life remain outside the law,

> particularly in . . . politics and policymaking, where reliance is placed on the nonrational, non-legal factors of force and violence, on the one hand, and of moral unity and common faith on the other. The personality of rulers still plays a dominant role, and personal influence is a crucial factor in impeding the movement for stability of laws.[105]

Western legalism, consequently, and its time-consuming "due process" have been disdained by many of Russia's intelligentsia, who have looked to personal and administrative relationships rather than to the formality of the law. As Nina Khrushcheva describes it:

> Such a country [Russia] established a set of values in mirror opposition to the West: Russian charity versus Western justice; order vs. law; trust vs. responsibility; nihilism and negation vs. competition; humanity vs. professionalism; truth vs. rules; faith vs. stimulus purpose; universalism vs. individualism; spirituality vs. interests, etc.[106]

Attempts in the late nineteenth and early twentieth centuries to establish a *Rechtsstaat,* a law-based state—Russians still use the German term—were only partially successful, due in part to the power of the tsar and a long tradition of arbitrary rule in disregard of the law. That tradition continued during the Soviet period when the state issued thousands of administrative regulations that were enforced by the authorities and the courts, even though many of them were in violation of the laws of the land. The Soviet judicial system, moreover, was subservient to the state, and a court's decision, particularly in the provinces, was often influenced by a telephone call to the presiding judge from a local Communist Party official, a practice known as *telefonoye pravo* (telephone law).

In civil law, a citizen could generally expect a fair trial, although the interests of the state were often given priority. In criminal law, however, acquittals were rare. As in Western Europe, but unlike the United States and the United Kingdom, a trial was required in Russia even if the accused pleaded guilty, as he or she did in some 90 percent of the cases. Of the remaining cases, only about one in ten resulted in acquittal. The judge, assisted by two assessors (lay judges), played a stronger role than in U.S. or British courts, acting as an interrogator together with the prosecutor rather than as a neutral umpire. In criminal law, until new legislation was passed in 1989, defense lawyers were often unable to obtain access to imprisoned defendants and their court records.

Exceptions to the law have been allowed, however, that permit the outcome sought by the courts and the state. Many laws are poorly drafted and vague. Also less than clear are the details of their operation, which are subject to administrative regulation. Laws are often passed but not enforced, and they are frequently overtaken by new legislation.

One aspect of law where Russia and the West differ most strikingly is that of individual rights. In the West, those rights are based on constitutions and laws that spell out the rights of individuals and the limits of state infringement on those rights. To Russians, however, rigorous application of the law to defend individuals may appear unduly legalistic. They would rather judge each situation in the light of circumstances, as in the mir, and weigh the relative interests of the individual and the community, a contest in which community interests may prevail.

Individual rights, moreover, may clash with the communal ethic. Russians are prejudiced against those who live differently or better than their neighbors. And in a culture that values harmony of thought and communal good, persons who differ from the established order are suspect. *Individualysty* (individualists)—which has a pejorative meaning in Russian—appear opposed to the sense of community as the basis for social good.

In Russia today there is again talk of a Rechtsstaat, and progress in achieving it has been enhanced by a program of judicial reform personally promoted by Putin, signed by him on December 17, 2001, and approved by the State Duma with the support of all political parties. The reforms affect all courts, including the *arbitrazh* (commercial) courts, which deal with disputes both between firms, and between firms and the government.

This legislation is intended to strengthen the independence and authority of judges, many of whom in the past were regarded as incompetent and were subject to outside pressures, while also reducing their immunity from prosecution and making them subject to discipline.[107] Appointments of judges are no longer screened by local legislatures—a procedure that made judges subject to influence by local politicians and their wealthy friends—but by a Qualification Commission of judges, lawyers, legal scholars, and Kremlin officials, which reviews appointments, promotions, removals from office, and punishments. Except for those of the Constitutional Courts, judges are to be appointed for six-year terms, not for unlimited terms as in the past, and the same person cannot be appointed as presiding or deputy presiding judge in the same court more than twice in a row.

This legislation also forces judges to retire at age 65 for regular courts and at 70 for higher courts. They can also be disciplined and face criminal charges or administrative punishment at the request of the prosecutor general and, if so decided, by a panel of three Supreme Court judges and with the consent of the Supreme Qualification Commission. To inhibit bribery, a dramatic increase in funding provides judges with increased salaries, additional staff, computerization of court proceedings, repair of court buildings, and interest-free and forgivable loans to enable new judges to buy homes.

The reforms of 2001 give judges the task of supervising pretrial investigations and call for more adversarial trials, but prosecutorial bias has not disappeared, as demonstrated by the low rates of acquittal. In 2002–2003, trial by jury was extended as an option to all those accused and facing trial at regional courts (except in Chechnya), and the rate of acquittal has averaged close to 20 percent. While the Supreme Court has overruled some of those acquittals, sending the cases for retrial, more than 10 percent of the accused in trial by jury have gained acquittals that have lasted. However, instances of specially chosen juries and of attempts to influence the positions of individual jurors have been reported in the press, and Russia's readiness for jury trials has been questioned.

Jury trials, nevertheless, are likely to last because of their position in the Constitution of the Russian Federation, which few politicians are willing to open for amendments. Jury trials also involve a higher standard of evidence than trials by judges alone, and they dramatize the accusatory bias in Russian criminal justice.

Despite these reforms, the continued attempts to influence judges reflect the legal and political culture beyond the world of the courts. All too often, leaders of government and business alike treat law as an instrument of power, while relying upon informal means to achieve their goals within formal institutions like courts. Paradoxically, both practices lead them to expect that judges will cooperate with their needs.

However, within the Russian Federation today there are variations among the more European and Asian parts of the country, reflecting different traditions and different balances in the importance of formal versus informal institutions. Whereas in some locations there might be a handful of cases a year involving attempted political influence, in others there might be dozens. The prevalence of payments to judges (with or without implications for the result of the trial) also vary markedly by region, court, and judge.[108]

The new legislation also introduced other reforms intended to provide a balance between the rights of lawyers and prosecutors. The authority of the previously all-powerful prosecutors has been curbed; their power to issue arrest and search warrants has been transferred to the courts, where they will now have to prove their cases with hard evidence or face acquittals by skeptical juries. In criminal cases, the participation of defense lawyers will be mandatory, although they will still need the approval of prosecutors to call witnesses. Defendants will be able to admit guilt and avoid a trial.

These reforms have been welcomed by Russian liberals and legal experts, but it remains to be seen how, and to what extent, they will be implemented in the coming years. In any event, most experts believe that the development of truly strong and respected courts in Russia will take decades, not years.

Nevertheless, 15 years of judicial reform in the Russian Federation have put into place the main institutional prerequisites for judicial independence, including security of tenure, decent salaries for judges, and adequate funding of the courts. As a result, judges in Russia feel more independent than before and are in a position to act impartially in most cases. At the same time, though, many judges do remain subject to pressure and attempts at influence in the small number of cases that matter to authorities or powerful persons, and there are also systemic biases that affect adjudication in criminal cases. Although some judges resist pressure and sometimes even biases, others cooperate, mainly because of the demands of a judicial career.[109]

Many international law firms have opened offices in Moscow, and they appear to function remarkably well in representing the interests of their clients, both foreign and Russian. The problem, as many foreign law firms point out, is not too little law in Russia, but too much, reflecting the highly regulated character of Soviet society that the new Russia has inherited.

Establishing a new company can take months and involves registering with several local and national government bodies. A law, "On the State Registration of Juridical Persons," intended to simplify and expedite procedures for registering a small business, was signed by Putin on July 1, 2001, but its application by officials has varied greatly across Russia according to the whims of the local bureaucracies.[110]

Foreign law firms, nevertheless, are generally satisfied with the progress made in judicial reform. As London's *Financial Times* has reported, one British law firm went to court in Moscow against a company closely linked to the FSB (the former KGB) and won. "Partly as a result of such cases," wrote *The Times*,

> the high commercial court in Moscow has a relatively good reputation for fairness. While the system is open to pressures—which some claim are getting worse as the current government looks to boost revenues—foreign investors appear generally pleased with the protection they receive. They say Russia is different from some parts of Asia, where being foreign means you will probably lose.[111]

Echoing that idea, Alexandra Nesterenko, head of legal affairs in Moscow for Unilever, the Anglo-Dutch consumer products company, says she does not feel the company's foreign ownership has ever made a difference in Russian courts although, she adds, "You can win a case and get the judgment but you cannot guarantee that you will get enforcement as a result."[112]

That view is seconded by Peter H. Solomon Jr., professor of political science and law at the University of Toronto, who writes:

> The greatest problems facing the courts in Russia in 2007 did not lie in the infrequent incidents of attempted political influence, but in the difficulty faced by victorious plaintiffs in securing implementation of civil judgments. The formal European style system of bailiff-executors based in an executive branch agency succeeded in collecting debts from noncooperating respondents barely half of the time, prompting some firms to rely on private enforcement agencies.[113]

Nevertheless, as Solomon points out:

> The late Putin years witnessed less real political competition than did the Yeltsin period, but democratic development often moves in cycles or zigs and zags. The current efforts to build modern and effective courts are laying the groundwork for judges who can act in a fully impartial way in the future, when larger political and institutional developments become more favorable.[114]

As an American lawyer with many years of experience in Russian courts puts it:

> Much has also been written about corruption in the Russian judiciary, and the alleged inability to get a fair hearing and treatment before the Russian courts. Certainly, corruption and political influence exist, and can be determinative in some cases, particularly where a strong political element is involved. But politically motivated cases, while highly visible, represent a very small portion of the cases actually litigated, and corruption is by no means omnipresent. From the standpoint of practicing commercial lawyers advising clients on doing business in Russia, therefore, the real picture is much less black and white than Western press reports would suggest. Our firm has litigated literally hundreds of Russian court and administrative cases over the past 15 years, ranging from tax, to construction, land and property, bankruptcy, intellectual property, consumer protection, antimonopoly and general commercial disputes, and the vast majority have been successfully prosecuted.[115]

ORDER AND DISORDER

[Russia] . . . this most anarchic of nations.

> —Francine du Plessix Gray, *Soviet Women*

Germans are known for their *Ordnung* (order) and Russians for their *besporyadok* (disorder). Yet order and disorder coexist in Russia, a fact of life to which visitors from the West will have to reconcile themselves. In Russian literature it is Germans who demonstrate order, discipline, and efficiency. The classic example is Stolz, in Ivan Goncharov's novel *Oblomov,* who is a model man of action, while Oblomov, his Russian opposite and friend, is a man of inaction who spends the first 50 pages of the novel getting out of bed in the morning. Oblomov is a favorite character of Russians, who see something of themselves in his inaction and disorder. It was not by chance that many high officials, diplomats, and military officers of Tsarist Russia were ethnic Germans from Russia's Baltic territories. Indeed, Russia's hardworking and businesslike current Prime Minister Putin has been described as "The German in the Kremlin."[116]

The Russian desire for order arises from the need of her rulers to bring a measure of discipline to an unruly people and marshal their productive potential for the security and well-being of state and society. Disorder derives from the anarchic strain in Russians, their rebellion against regimentation, defiance of authority, flouting of regulations when they believe they can safely do so, and disinclination to plan ahead.

Russians may respect authority, but they are not intimidated by it. Seeing themselves as coequal with others, they are not shy about speaking up in public or asserting themselves. Nor are they hesitant about forcefully requesting things that they believe are rightly theirs or that they would like to possess. Persistent and tenacious, they rarely accept no for an answer.

Westerners who arrive at Moscow's Sheremetyevo Airport—built by Germans—are struck by the confusion, in contrast to the efficiency of West European airports. By Soviet standards, however, Sheremetyevo is well run because it is a gateway to the country and was built to serve foreign travelers. The further one travels from Moscow, the greater the airport confusion.

One winter night in 1988, I changed planes in Sverdlovsk (now Yekaterinburg), a Siberian city on the eastern slope of the Ural Mountains. The third largest city in Russia, and Boris Yeltsin's hometown and former fiefdom, it was closed to foreigners at the time. In fact, I must have been one of the first Americans in Sverdlovsk since U-2 pilot Gary Powers unexpectedly deplaned there in 1960. A major industrial center with a regional population of more than three million, Sverdlovsk had no Intourist facilities and no services for foreign travelers. (Sverdlovsk was not officially opened to foreigners until 1991.)

The Sverdlovsk air terminal recalled scenes of New York's Grand Central Station during rush hour. A large crowd jammed the concourse. The public address system was barely intelligible. There were no seats and no places to rest except the restrooms, which also had no seats.

When my flight was called, late as usual, there was the familiar pushing and shoving at the flight gate, not unlike a rugby scrum. After passengers were finally corralled into a small holding area and left standing, jammed together like sardines, there were more unexplained delays. When a bus eventually delivered us to the plane's ramp, we were left to wait another half hour in the frigid Siberian night while the plane was being readied. Between flight gate and plane ramp, tickets and identity documents of all passengers had been checked three times. Control was the primary concern of the airport officials, as it has been of all Russian governments.

Russian governments have traditionally had two main tasks, wrote Berkeley's Martin Malia—to maintain order internally and to wage war externally.[117] Maintaining internal order meant keeping the peasants in line, since they were some 90 percent of the population. Without a strong hand to guide them, both tsars and commissars believed that the unruly Russians would quickly descend into anarchy.

Communism strove to overcome Russian disorder by introducing rationalism and by planning and regimentation. "Try to understand the regimented way in which we live," a Russian teacher explained to me. "Things here are either yes or no, with no shades of interpretation in between."

There are regulations for everything. Uniformed *militsia* (police) are seen everywhere in the cities, controlling pedestrian as well as motor vehicle traffic, and enforcing regulations that often do not make sense. Jaywalking is strictly forbidden, and violators risk being cited by the militsia. Ronald Hingley relates how beachmasters at Black Sea resorts would blow whistles to command sunbathers to turn over at intervals so as to avoid sunburn (a command ignored by the sun-loving Russians).[118]

What should you do if you are stopped by the militsia for some minor infringement? My recommendation is to keep talking without raising your voice, admit to your transgression if you are clearly in the wrong—confession may bring absolution—but also explain any extenuating circumstances. You can't beat city hall, in Russia as in the West, but the militsia can have a heart if appealed to on a personal level, if their authority is not questioned, and if slipped a little something on the side.

Russians drive on the right side of the road, and motor vehicles are not allowed to make left turns unless there is a traffic light with a green arrow. To turn left, drivers must proceed to a designated point where a *razvorot* (U-turn) may be made (very cautiously). It is only two blocks from Spaso House, the U.S. ambassador's residence in Moscow, to the Ministry of Foreign Affairs, but to get there by car in my years in Moscow, the ambassador had to drive more than a mile, making two U-turns along a circuitous route.

Returning to Moscow once with my family by rail from the West, I purchased a basket of food in Vienna to sustain us over the 36-hour journey, since there was no dining car on the Soviet leg of the route. At Brest, the Polish-Soviet border crossing, a diligent Russian agricultural inspector rummaged through our food basket. Spying the bananas, she warned us that they could not be brought into the country. (Whether this was to protect the local banana crop was not made clear.) "What to do?" I asked. "Eat them," she replied. So my children ate the bananas and brought the peels into Russia without objection.

Order is also valued because Russians believe it helps to provide a clear view of the future and thus avoids the uncertainty of the present that they so dislike. Communism played on this fear of the unknown by promising everything for the future but failing to deliver. That penchant for predicting the future and revising the past—rewriting the history books—has given rise to many jokes. According to one *anekdot,* Russians know the future; it's the past they are not sure of.

Despite the many regulations and the many officials to enforce them, Russia appears disorderly to the Westerner. As the Marquis de Custine described it in 1839, "Every thing is here done by fits and starts, or with exceptions—a capricious system, which too often accords with the irregulated minds of the people. . . ."[119] Eighty-five years later, Lenin expressed a similar view:

> It is simply the usual Russian intellectual inability to do practical things—inefficiency and lackadaisicalness. First they bustle around, do something, and then think about it, and when nothing comes of it, they run to complain . . . and want the matter brought up before the Political Bureau.[120]

Waste is widespread. In 1990, 40 million tons of grain were lost at harvest time, roughly equal to the amount of grain the Soviet Union had to import from the West in that year.[121] Spills of crude oil, Russia's largest foreign-currency earner, are estimated at 10–18 percent of total annual output.[122] Grandiose projects are begun and left unfinished. Wherever people congregate, there is an aura of disarray.

"Russia's chronic chaos," writes Serge Schmemann in *The New York Times,* "is both its burden and its strength. Few nations could have endured what Russia has gone through in the last decade without a total breakdown."[123]

But despite their manifest disorder, Russians appreciate the need for order, and many of them who visit the United States are confused by what they regard as the disorder of America. How can there be such abundance without a plan, central control, and a strong leader? How can there be national direction and unity of purpose with so many political views, religions, and discordant voices? And how can democracy, seen by many Russians as itself a manifestation of disorder, result in such strength and material abundance?

"In the United States," writes Rachel Connell, who spent a year in Russia as an exchange student, "when you follow the directions carefully . . . nine times out of ten things will work out as planned. . . . In Russia people are suspicious of something they receive without a hassle."[124]

SCHOOL DAYS, RULE DAYS

The Soviet school encouraged conformity and political docility, and generally suppressed initiative as well as independent thought.
—Ben Eklof and Edward Dneprov, *Democracy in the Russian School*

All of us have been formed by the schools we have attended, but Russians even more so. Many of the Russian characteristics described in earlier chapters have been reinforced by the schools Russians attended when they were young and by the Soviet system of education. It is therefore to the Soviet schools of the past that we must look in order to better understand the adult Russians whom we will be encountering today.

"Authorities in the Soviet state understood very well," wrote Canadian child education specialist Landon Pearson, "that the school is the most important social institution that exists outside the family for shaping the social and moral development of children."[125] To ensure that children would be shaped according to the needs of the Soviet state and the Communist Party, Soviet education was known for its excessive centralization, authoritarian approaches, piled-on homework, rote learning in large classrooms, and orientation of the pupil toward the collective rather than the individual. Nevertheless, as the well-known American author Susan Jacoby has pointed out, the atmosphere in individual schools could vary widely, and some dedicated school principals and teachers were able to moderate many of those Party-driven practices.[126]

Schools of the Soviet era had roots in the Russian past. Russian schools traditionally have been more than places to learn reading, writing, and 'rithmetic; they have also been tasked with moral education—the character building that Russians call *vospitaniye* (upbringing). In a Russian version of civic education, schools were to teach children how to behave and relate to others in society.

Another Russian tradition, in force since the nineteenth century, was using uniform curricula and textbooks in an effort to homogenize its far-flung imperium. As Pearson illustrated:

It used to be possible . . . for a youngster to close his geography book in Moscow one morning, fly the long distance to Novosibirsk that afternoon for an extended visit to his grandfather, go to school the next day, and find his new class studying the same page he had left the day before.[127]

The Soviet school, like the Russian school before it, strongly reflected old European education traditions—centralization, the authority of the teacher, and a rather formal curriculum with few or no electives. The Soviets continued those traditions and added a few more. An extensive system of public schools blanketed the country, eliminated illiteracy, and raised the general level of learning among the populace. Vospitaniye continued in the schools but was manipulated to encourage conformity and serve the needs of the state. Indoctrination of political and social values began in kindergarten and continued through the school years in an effort to form a new "Soviet person" better able to contribute to the building of socialism.

The Soviet theory of education was deeply influenced in the 1930s by Anton Makarenko, an influential but controversial educator who had worked for many years to rehabilitate and educate the homeless, the delinquent, and juveniles. Makarenko's theories dominated Soviet education until the late 1950s. The child was to be educated as a member of a collective organized along semimilitary lines and instilled with respect for the authority of the collective and of the person chosen to lead it. From their earliest years, pupils were taught to think and act collectively, respect the authority of the teacher, and observe the rules of the classroom. (In Russia, the word uchenik (pupil) is used for those in primary and secondary schools, while student, as elsewhere in Europe, is reserved for those in higher education.)

"A respectful and, indeed, slightly fearful attitude to adult authority," wrote Pearson, "is inculcated into Soviet children from the moment they set foot into an educational establishment. The degree of respect (and fear) increases with the age and status of the older person."[128]

Teachers taught the required curriculum with little concern for the individual needs of pupils. Discipline was strict, and there was little or no discussion in the classroom. For each question by the teacher there was one correct answer, and pupils soon learned that knowing the "right" answer would ensure good grades, which in turn would lead to admission to a university, a good job, and the perks that the state offered its educated elites.

In their first year of school, all pupils joined the Octobrists, their first collective, where as a group they performed socially useful activities such as classroom cleanup, critiqued their classmates' attitudes toward learning, and heard lectures on Lenin and the Soviet Motherland. In their third year they became Young Pioneers, and the level of group activity and political indoctrination increased. At age fourteen, most joined the Komsomol (Young Communist League), the prelude to Party membership. Peer pressure to join, as well as penalties for failure to do so, often proved difficult to resist. After

1985 the popularity of these organizations declined, and they were disbanded in 1991.

Economic demands also shaped education, alternating between two conflicting needs of the state. An expanding economy required better educated workers, which called for more years of schooling. But as the economy expanded and productivity declined, more workers were needed, which required reducing the time spent in school and moving graduates more rapidly into the workforce. The result was a back-and-forth of policy changes and reforms between general education, which prepared pupils for entrance to higher education (universities and colleges), and general education combined with vocational training, which produced the expanded labor force.

The system essentially had two tracks. Some pupils completed ten years of general education and went on to higher schools. Others ended their general education after eight years and transferred to vocational schools that trained future workers and paraprofessionals, or else they then went to specialized secondary schools that prepared graduates for skilled occupations as well as for higher education in industrial fields. Education was compulsory, free of charge, and coeducational. Schooling began at age seven and continued for ten years, four to six hours a day, five or six days a week. The conflict between general education and vocational training was temporarily resolved by adding another school year, for a total of eleven, but that was done by starting school one year earlier, at age six. And in a concession to advocates of vocational training, pupils in all schools were required to learn a trade that would qualify them for employment.

As educators and society imposed more and more demands on the schools, many of them became overcrowded and had to resort to second and even third shifts, so that many children began and ended their school day quite late. The curricula became overloaded, and homework more time-consuming. Few teachers and pupils could complete the state-mandated requirements, thus producing a false record of achievement and a tradition of lip service rather than genuine assimilation of knowledge.

Higher education was little different, as former Minister of Education Yevgeny Tkachenko explained:

> I spent my whole life in higher education. We ... were not allowed to change not only the sequence of courses, but even to reduce by one hour the time allocated to some subject. We lived in the tight Procrustean bed of study plans stipulated for us by the Central Committee of the party, and we were not allowed to deviate even by a single step to the right or to the left.[129]

By the end of the 1990s, however, changes began to be made as a reform movement pushed slowly ahead, and control of the schools, as well as financial responsibility for them, was transferred to local authorities.[130] Curricula were revised, new textbooks written, the education system decentralized, local initiative in education encouraged, teachers' pay increased, and private schools permitted. The once-obligatory school uniforms are no longer mandated by the state, although some schools may still require them, and political propaganda has been removed from the classroom and replaced by a more democratic and humane environment. Some electives have been added, and Saturday classes were discontinued in many districts.

Military training, however, which had been removed from the curriculum in 1991, was reinstated in 2000. Under a decree issued by Putin, schoolboys age fifteen and older are now given premilitary training to prepare them for service in the armed forces. Schoolgirls, in a resumption of traditional Russian gender roles, are taught basic medical techniques for helping soldiers wounded in battle.

But many obstacles to reform remain. In addition to resistance by an entrenched bureaucracy, schools are still dismally underfunded, and there are shortages of textbooks, teachers, and treasure. Teachers are still poorly paid, their morale is low, and local authorities do not always have the funds to pay salaries and provide the necessary resources that teachers need. Almost everywhere, parents must make sizeable contributions to school maintenance at the start of the school year, and sometimes during the year, to help pay for emergency expenses.

Decentralization of schools during the 1990s, however, has given school principals and teachers the freedom to try out their own teaching techniques, especially in the new private schools that have proliferated. Change is coming to Russian schools, and they will be different from the schools of the Soviet era, which many of today's adults attended. The changes, however, will be slow in coming since half of all graduates of teacher training institutions never enter a schoolroom after graduating, and many of today's teachers are staying on longer to earn their pensions.

Today, four years of primary education are followed by five of "incomplete" secondary education. After those nine years, about half of all pupils complete two more years of general secondary education in preparation for higher education. The others transfer either to vocational schools or specialized secondary schools. Parental pressure, however, has increased the demand for higher education and its rewards, and since the 1970s it has also been possible for graduates of vocational schools to advance to higher education.

For the gifted and talented there are state schools specializing in math, science, and the arts. Other schools specialize in foreign languages, producing graduates who are nearly bilingual.

With no formal division between primary school, incomplete secondary, and secondary school, pupils in the general education track remain in the same building with the same classmates, often in the same home room, throughout all 11 years of school, forging strong bonds of friendship with classmates, as well as loyalties to teachers, that last throughout life. Many of the friends and familiar faces with whom Russians feel so comfortable and secure are based on those old school ties. Putin, for example, was instrumental in getting a better apartment for his old secondary school teacher of German, even though she was living in Israel at the time.[131]

Applicants to institutions of higher learning take oral and written exams at the end of the ninth and eleventh years, as well as entrance exams given by higher-education institutions. Some 20 percent of those ages 18 to 21 are enrolled in colleges and universities, but that figure includes many who are enrolled in evening or extension courses rather than studying full-time.

Competition for entrance to elite institutions is very keen, and nepotism, influence, and bribery are widespread. But there is no gender discrimination in admissions, and the numbers of male and female students are about equal. Women, however, predominate in the humanities, medicine, and education, a result more of traditional Russian notions of "female occupations" than overt discrimination.

Getting good grades in school and being admitted to higher education is important for young men as a way of avoiding or postponing military service, which is mandatory at age 18. University students are automatically given a deferment, thereby avoiding military service with its hazing, humiliation, and degradation.

Higher education institutions each year formerly reserved a number of places for so-called "commercial students," who may not have had the high grades necessary for admission but were able to pay a substantial tuition fee.[132] As a result, students with lower grades who could pay were admitted, while students with good grades who could not pay the higher fee were not admitted and had to serve in the military.

To correct that inequity, the Russian parliament in 2007 approved a Unified State Examination, a standardized test, so that admission to higher education would be based solely on academic results rather than the ability to pay. The new exam, similar to the German *Abitur,* French *Baccalaureate,* British General Certificate of Secondary Education (GCSE), and American Scholastic Aptitude Test (SAT), will replace both the *Vypustnoi Examen* (graduating exam) of Russian secondary schools as well as the admission exams offered by many universities.

The broad liberal arts education leading to a bachelor's degree, as in the United Kingdom and the United States, was unknown in the Soviet Union. Rather, higher education was narrowly specialized to produce graduates in professions needed by the economy. On applying to a university or higher school, students had to choose their major field of study, and that choice would determine whether they were accepted. For decades, a quota for the number of first-year students in each field of study was set by future needs of the economy as determined by the five-year economic plans. For example, the projected need for petroleum engineers five years hence would determine the number of students allowed to enter the five-year study program in petroleum engineering. That practice, however, has been moderated in recent years, and institutions of higher education now have increased flexibility in determining their enrollments.

As a sign of the changing times, in 2003 Russia signed on to the Bologna Convention, under which higher education throughout Europe is being standardized, equivalencies established, and structures and practices made more uniform, so that degrees in one country will be recognized in the others.

As a step in that direction, in 2007 Russia announced changes in its organization of higher education. Under legislation signed by then President Putin, higher education will be reorganized into two levels.[133] The first level, taking three to four years depending on the area of study, will lead to a bachelor's degree. The second level, two additional years, will lead to a master's degree. The undergraduate program will prepare students for executive positions in industrial or socio-economic work. Graduate programs will prepare students for analytical, design, and research activities. Specialist courses of five to six years will continue for some areas, such as health care and state security.

First-year students are formed into *gruppy* (groups) within each department. With few electives, students remain in those groups with the same classmates through their undergraduate years, a continuation of the group bonding that began in primary school. The length of study for future teachers with one specialization is four years, but most take a fifth year and specialize in two disciplines. Most other students also study five years, earning the degree of certified specialist. Medical doctors study six years, followed by an internship and residency.

Graduate study, the *aspirantura,* is three years and leads to the *Kandidat nauk* (candidate of sciences) degree, somewhat short of a Western doctorate. Full professors usually have the full doctorate, generally considered higher than a Western Ph.D. and awarded after additional research.

Instruction is largely theoretical and highly specialized. Students attend lectures and take notes but rarely challenge their professors. Russian students excel in mathematics and science, but the system generally does not produce well-rounded graduates who are able to respond to the challenges of technological change they will face in the workplace. Russian universities, moreover, emphasize teaching. Research, for the most part, is the preserve of the various academies of science, which also award academic degrees, but they have been suffering from state neglect and underfunding. The separation of teaching and research is a shortcoming of Russian higher education and a recognized handicap for both students and professors.

Respect for teachers and professors continues. Some university professors still expect their students to rise when the professor enters the classroom, and a student will address a professor by his or her first name and patronymic, but never by the first name alone.

Russian educators who have visited Western schools have been impressed by the sophisticated equipment, the libraries, and the laboratories, and they have also noted the interaction between students and teachers, the encouragement of independent thinking rather than rote learning, the wide choice of electives, independent study, the self-reliance of students, and the responsibility they assume for their own education. At the same time, shifts in Russian public opinion have recently brought renewed respect for the "Russian tradition" in education and diminished interest in U.S. schools. Many Russians continue to believe that their schools are the best in the world, even while Program for International Student Assessment (PISA) surveys of pupil achievement in dozens of countries have ranked Russian schools poorly in terms of basic skills in several areas.

Russian education, however, does have its strengths. Russian immigrants in the United States have learned that their children are two to three years ahead of American pupils in math and science, and they are also more knowledgeable about literature and history. This is due largely to their Russian teachers who, although poorly paid, were well prepared and dedicated. It may also be because so many immigrants are from families with higher education and a tradition for learning.

FIVE

Personal Encounters

Russians are more emotional, more likely to strike deep friendships, less super-ficially gregarious. They make great sacrifices for those within their trusted cir-cle, and they expect real sacrifices in return. Their willingness, indeed their eagerness, to engage at a personal level makes private life in Russia both enor-mously rich and incredibly entangling. Close emotional bonds are part of Rus-sia's enchantment and also its complexity.

—Hedrick Smith, *The New Russians*

THE CITY

The city itself in Russia is an implanted thing, and . . . the urban man who has created the civilizations of the West is still in the making here. His habit-ual loneliness, his totally private life, his ignorance of his neighbors, his go-it-alone psychology—these are still in conflict in Russia with an older way of communal existence.

—Inge Morath and Arthur Miller, *In Russia*

First-time visitors to Russia will be struck—literally as well as figuratively—by the large crowds of people they encounter and the ever-present body con-tact. Russian cities swarm with people.

Forced industrialization moved masses of peasants from the warm and personal environment of their native villages to the cold and impersonal surroundings of large cities. Between 1926 and 1939, the Moscow and Leningrad regions grew by 3,500,000 each.[134]

There is no real analogy in the United States (or other countries), as Inge Morath and Arthur Miller point out, although Americans can look back to something similar in their own cities in the days before World War I

> when the cities were filling up with country people who had to learn to be up-to-date, to forget the ideas of mutual help . . . and to relate themselves to an impersonal administration rather than to officials they knew and to personalities they understood and who understood them.[135]

Most urban residents in Russia are only one, two, or three generations removed from their ancestral villages and peasant traditions. As Ronald Hingley describes them, ". . . even in the towns—in Moscow or Tula, say—a Russian crowd seems to react in a more peasant-like manner, however defined, than would be the case in Rome, Munich or Pittsburgh."[136] The cities became "ruralized," writes Stites, ". . . imbued with peasant values— at home, on the streets, and at work. Urban civilization did not efface rural mentalities; rather, the opposite occurred."[137] Residents of St. Petersburg, however, will argue today that people are more polite in *Piter,* as their more European city is affectionately called.

Despite the dislocations derived from their move from village to city, Russians regard urban life as infinitely better than rural life. In the city there are new opportunities not only for work but also for education, culture, and recreation. Housing and municipal services, however, have not kept pace with the large influx of new residents.

Most city dwellers live in small apartments in large multistoried buildings rather than in detached houses. But because of the continuing housing shortage, as well as a real estate boom resulting from the recent privatization of apartments, some Russians still live in a *kommunalka* (communal apartment), one family occupying one or two rooms while sharing a kitchen and bathroom with one or more other families. The need to find relief from indoor crowding is one reason why so many Russians are seen on the streets.

Stores and markets these days are full of food and consumer goods— albeit at prices many cannot afford, due to rising inflation. The soaring food prices are a particular worry in Russia, where many still live in poverty.

Food costs consume the bulk of many household incomes, and memories of food shortages and rationing are still fresh in people's minds.

Unmet demands can make Russians very aggressive about trying to acquire things they want but do not have or cannot afford, and they are not at all bashful about making such requests to foreign visitors who may be put off by their persistence. A first response of "no" is never accepted as final. Believing that every response can be manipulated and changed, Russians will repeat their requests over and over again, adding a new twist each time.

Requests may be for medicines not available, scholarships to foreign universities, books or laboratory equipment required for research, or assistance in emigrating. Visitors will need to be patient in rebuffing requests that they cannot or do not wish to fulfill. They should also not make promises they cannot keep or agree to miracles they cannot perform.

One type of request that visitors can easily fulfill is to help Russians establish contact with professional counterparts abroad. Russians will seek names and addresses of people or organizations in their profession or in fields in which they have a personal interest. The intent is to establish contact and exchange information with the outside world, which was difficult to do in the Soviet era.

Others may wish to locate relatives abroad. One Russian I met in the middle of Siberia, whose Texas-born father had emigrated to the Soviet Union during the Depression, had been trying for years, without success, through both U.S. and Soviet government channels, to find his long-lost American relatives. On my return home, I was able to locate several of his family members who had been trying for years to locate their Russian cousin. For that Russian, I was indeed a miracle maker.

Large crowds make municipal authorities apprehensive, and their response is crowd control. Uniformed police, the militsia (*police* was considered a capitalist term), are ever present in Russian cities. At sports events and other activities that attract large crowds, long convoys of militsia trucks may be parked nearby in case a crowd gets unruly or out of control, as occasionally occurs. In 1982, at a soccer match in Moscow's Luzhniki stadium, some 340 fans were crushed to death by a surging crowd.[138] And more than 500 people were suffocated or trampled to death on Moscow streets in 1953 when Stalin's body lay in state.[139] It is prudent to stay on the fringes of large crowds to avoid being swept away and trampled.

Russians do not always queue up naturally, as do Americans and West Europeans. Rather than line up and patiently await their turn, Russians will at times storm buildings and box offices—pushing, shoving, and elbowing—determined to gain access or obtain their share before whatever they seek is gone. At airports, even when all passengers are ticketed and have reservations, Russians will throng around the flight gate and plane ramp, anxious lest they not be boarded.

At popular concerts and sports events, persons without tickets have been known to storm the gate in an attempt to gain admission. Such storming is done not only by the *narod* (common people) but also by the intelligentsia. I witnessed one such *Sturm und Drang* when music students stormed the entrance to the Moscow Conservatory Great Hall, seeking admission to a performance of Bach's *Passion According to St. John* by a visiting West German ensemble. Bach was rarely performed in Russia at that time, and the hall had been sold out in advance to music lovers with connections.

FRIENDS AND FAMILIAR FACES

Better to have one hundred friends than one hundred rubles.

—Russian proverb

The value of the Russian ruble may increase or decrease but not the value of Russian friends. Friends and familiar faces are the key to getting things done in Russia, and foreigners who cultivate close relationships will have a big advantage in doing business there.

Sol Hurok, the legendary American impresario who pioneered North American tours by Soviet dance and music groups, would visit the Soviet Union periodically to audition performing artists and to select those he would sign for performances abroad. Traveling alone, Hurok would negotiate and sign contracts for extensive U.S. coast-to-coast tours by such large ensembles as the Bolshoi Ballet and the Moscow Philharmonic.

On one such visit to Moscow in 1969, when Hurok was 80 years old, I asked him how he could sign contracts for such large and costly undertakings without lawyers and others to advise him. "I have been coming here for many years and doing business with the Russians," he replied confidently. "I simply write out a contract by hand on a piece of paper, and we both sign it. They know and trust me."

A similar but more recent experience is reported by William McCulloch, an American whose business activities in Russia include housing construction and telecommunications. The key to doing business in Russia, says

McCulloch, is finding the right partner—one with whom a basis of trust is established over time. "You cannot bring in an army of New York lawyers and have an ironclad deal. You have to have a clear understanding with the right partner about what you are doing." Such an understanding, he adds, makes it possible to negotiate one's way through the Russian political, economic, and banking systems.[140]

A different experience is reported by an American who met with a group of people from various parts of Russia to help form a national coalition in support of democracy. Assembled in the room were persons with a common purpose and a shared commitment to democracy. Yet, in their first meeting it became apparent that their loyalties were to their local organizations, each with its own parochial interests, and not to the broad coalition and platform they hoped to forge. Suspicious of each other, they were reluctant to speak up in public. They also did not trust the interpreter, a Russian whom the American had brought with him. Many more meetings were required before the American, by talking with the participants individually and in small groups, and eating, drinking, and socializing with them, was able to overcome their initial distrust, not only of him but of their fellow Russians, and eventually help them to forge a viable coalition.

Russians rely on a close network of family, friends, and coworkers as protection against the risks and unpredictability of daily life. In the village commune, Russians felt safe and secure in the company of family and neighbors. Today, in the city, they continue to value familiar faces and mistrust those they do not know.

Visitors who know a Russian from a previous encounter will have a big advantage. First-time travelers to Russia are advised to ask friends who already know the people they will be meeting to put in a good word for them in advance of their visits. And ideally the same traveler should return for subsequent visits and not be replaced by someone else from the firm or organization whose turn has come for a trip to Russia.

Despite its vast size, or perhaps because of it, Russia is run on the basis of personal connections. In both the workplace and in private life, Russians depend on those they know—friends who owe them favors, former classmates, fellow military veterans, and others whom they trust. The bureaucracy is not expected to respond equitably to a citizen's request. Instead, Russians will call friends and ask for their help.

The friendship network also extends to the business world. Business managers, short of essential parts or materials, will use their personal contacts to obtain the necessary items. Provide a spare part or commodity for someone, and receive something in return. Without such contacts, production would grind to a halt.

Westerners who want something from their government will approach the responsible official, state their case, and assume that law and logic will prevail. Russians in the same situation, mistrustful of the state and its laws, will approach friends and acquaintances and ask them to put in a good word with the official who will decide.

The process is reciprocal: those who do favors for Russians can expect favors in return. I once offered some friendly advice to a newly arrived Soviet cultural attaché in Washington on how to get things done in the United States. He returned the favor many times over, smoothing my way through the Moscow bureaucratic maze as we developed a mutually advantageous professional relationship. I was pleased to consider him a friend.

The word *friend,* however, must be used carefully in Russia. For most Americans, anyone who is not an enemy seems to be a friend. An American can become acquainted with a complete stranger and in the next breath will describe that person as a friend. American friendships, however, are compartmentalized, often centering around colleagues in an office, neighbors in a residential community, or participants in recreational activities. This reflects the American reluctance to get too deeply involved with the personal problems of others. A friend in need may be a friend indeed, but an American is more likely to refer a needy friend to a professional for help rather than become involved in the friend's personal troubles.

Not so with Russians, for whom friendship is all encompassing and connotes a special relationship. Dancer Mikhail Baryshnikov, when asked about the difference between Russian and American friendships, replied:

> In Russia, because the society has been so closed, you're sharing your inside with your friends. Your views on society. Political points of view. It's a small circle of people whom you trust. And you get so attached. Talking with friends becomes your second nature. A need. Like at 4 o'clock in the morning, without a phone call, your friend can come to your house, and you're up and putting the teapot on. That kind of friendship.[141]

The Russian language has different words for *friend* (*drug,* pronounced "droog") and *acquaintance* (*znakomy*), and these words should not be misused. A drug is more like a "bosom buddy," someone to trust, confide in, and treat like a member of the family. Such friendships are not made easily or quickly. They take time to develop, but when they are made and nurtured, a Russian friendship will embrace the entire person. Russians will ask friends for time and favors that most Americans would regard as impositions.

Friendship with a Russian is not to be treated lightly. One American describes it as smothering, and some will find that it is more than they can handle. As one Russian explained, "Between Russian friends, what's theirs is yours and what's yours is theirs, especially if it's in the refrigerator."

Americans tend to be informal in their speech—candid, direct, and without the rituals, polite forms, and indirect language common to many other cultures. Russians welcome and appreciate such informal talk, but usually only after a certain stage in the relationship has been reached.

Addressing an American or Briton presents a dilemma for Russians. Their language has equivalents for *Mr.* (*Gospodin*) and *Mrs.* (*Gospozha*), but until recently these were considered relics of the prerevolutionary past and were not in common use. Now, with the demise of communism, Russians may use these older terms of address in formal meetings.

The preferred form of address among Russians, however, and the one most likely to be used in the initial stage of a relationship, is the first name and patronymic (father's name plus an affix). For example, a man named Boris, whose father was Nikolai, is addressed as Boris Nikolayevich (Boris, son of Nicholas). Similarly, a woman named Mariya whose father was Fyodor (Theodore), would be Mariya Fyodorovna (with the feminine ending -*a*).[142] Use of the patronymic does not signify friendship but is less formal than "Mr." or "Ms." With the friendship stage comes the use of the first name by itself, or a nickname. But first-name usage with a foreigner does not necessarily indicate that the friendship stage has been reached, as it would with another Russian. It does signify, however, the next stage in a developing relationship.

Like most European languages, Russian has two forms of *you*. The more formal *vy* is used between strangers, acquaintances, and in addressing people of higher position. The informal *ty*, akin to the old English *thou* and the French *tu* or German *du*, is reserved for friends, family members, and children; it is also used in talking down to someone and addressing animals. Readers will surely appreciate the need for care in using the familiar form.

Which of these forms should you use in addressing Russians? That will depend on the state of the relationship, and it may differ in each case. When in doubt, let the Russians decide and follow their lead.

Carry a good supply of business cards (*vizitnaya*, from "visiting card"). Have them printed in English on one side and Russian (in Cyrillic) on the other. Be sure to include your title, academic degrees, and anything else that might impress.

AT HOME

At home do as you wish, but in public as you are told.

—Russian proverb

Russians live two separate and distinct lives—one at work and the other at home. At work they can be brusque and discourteous but will watch what they say. At home, within the intimate circle of family and friends, they feel secure and are relaxed, warm, and hospitable, are sharing and caring, and speak their own minds.

As Morath and Miller describe it:

There is still a homeliness about many Russians that has the scent of the country in it, a capacity for welcoming strangers with open, unabashed curiosity, a willingness to show feeling, and above all a carelessness about the passing of time.[143]

When asked what Russians were thinking during the many decades of political repression, legal scholar Nina Belyaeva explained:

People did not connect themselves with the power of the state. On the one hand, they seemed from outside not to care, so they seemed submissive. But inside, they said, "Inside, I am me. They can't touch me. When I'm in my kitchen with my friends, I am free."[144]

The kitchen is indeed the center of social life, and visitors should not pass up opportunities to get into those kitchens and see Russians at home. There is no better way to get to know Russians than over food and drink or merely sitting around a kitchen table sipping tea. And when hosting Russians in your own home, bear in mind that Russians will appreciate dining in the kitchen, which gives them the feeling they are being treated as "family" rather than as guests in a formal dining room.

"The secret of social life in Russia," says Stites, "is conviviality around a table, drinking, telling jokes, laughing. When you get to that point, the battle is half won."[145]

Hospitality is spontaneous and intrinsic to the culture. Russians will share what they have and make their guests feel at home. Dinner may be served in the kitchen or in a parlor that doubles as a bedroom. The dishes may not match and the table service will be informal, but the visitor will be made to feel welcome. Food will be tasty, and guests will wonder how the hosts could afford the many delicacies. As in most European countries, the hot meal is usually eaten in the middle of the day—the legacy of an agricultural society where sustenance was needed for work in the fields—and the evening meal is more like a supper. Today, however, the old rules no longer apply, and the big meal may be in early afternoon or evening. But whenever it takes place, a meal always begins with wishing others at the table *priyatnovo appetita,* an equivalent of the French *bon appétit.*

Friends and relatives may drop in unexpectedly and join the table. Spirits will flow, and the talk will be lively and natural. Conversation is a very important part of social life, and over food and drink Russians open up and reveal their innermost thoughts.

Describing conversations with Russians, Geoffrey Hosking writes, "the exchange and exploration of ideas proceeds [*sic*] with utter spontaneity and at the same time concentration. In my experience, the art of conversation is pursued in Moscow at a higher level than anywhere else in the world."[146]

Guests should observe an old custom and bring a gift. Be cautious, however, about expressing admiration for an object in a Russian home. In a spontaneous gesture of hospitality, the host may present the admired object to the guest, and the offer will be difficult to refuse.

Russians welcome inquiries about family and children, and they will be interested in learning about a visitor's family. Such interest is genuine and should not be seen as merely making small talk. The fastest way to a Russian host's heart is to speak frankly about personal matters—joys and sorrows, successes and failures—which show that you are a warm human being and not just another cold Westerner.

Family and children are important in Russian life, although society's current ills—housing, high prices, lack of privacy, crime, alcoholism, and divorce—have taken their toll. In cities, families with one child are the norm, and I was always surprised when Russians expressed admiration on learning that I was the father of three.

How visitors live is also of great interest. Bring photos of family, home, and recreational activities, which will all be of interest. Russians are curious about the lifestyles of others in professions and occupations similar to their own, and they will not hesitate to inquire about a visitor's salary or the cost of a home and how many rooms it has. When a celebrated Soviet writer visited my home in the Washington suburbs, I expected our talk to be about life and literature. Instead, the world-renowned author requested a tour of the house and had a series of questions about the heating, air conditioning, and insulation, how much everything cost, and whether the house was my year-round home or my weekend dacha.

A *dacha*, literally a summer cottage, is something every Russian, reflecting their attachment to the land, seems to have or want, and where they spend weekends, weather permitting. Dachas used to be little more than a small shack without electricity or running water but with a garden plot for growing vegetables, which sustained entire families when food was scarce. But they have gradually grown in size, depending on the resources of the owner and the availability of transport from the city. Today, for Russia's privileged a dacha may also be a substantial brick or masonry home with all the "conveniences" in a gated community surrounded by a fence and protected by armed guards.

Handshaking is required practice in Russia, both on arrival and taking leave, with eye contact maintained during the handshake. Men do not shake hands with a woman unless she extends hers first, and women should not be surprised if their hands are kissed rather than shaken. Shaking hands over a threshold, however, as mentioned earlier, is an omen of bad luck and should never be done. If you are a man, physical signs of affection toward your host (embracing or touching) are good, but show reserve toward his wife. She will not appreciate hugs and kisses but will welcome flowers—in odd numbers only, though, but not thirteen. Old superstitions survive, and an even number of flowers is considered unlucky.

Once over the threshold and into the home, you will likely encounter a cloud of smoke. The antismoking campaign has only recently reached Russia, and more than half of all men still smoke and are literally smoking themselves to death. Russia leads the world in tobacco consumption per head of household, and it holds first place for teenage smokers. From 1996 to 2006, the death rate from smoking-related illnesses rose from 250,000 to 400,000 deaths annually. That high death rate is due to the high content of tar and nicotine in Russian cigarettes, many of which are sold without filters.[147] In a small apartment or office with windows closed tight in winter, the smoke can be oppressive for nonsmokers. In mild weather you can request that a window be opened. Offer to remove your shoes, especially in winter or inclement weather. Russians do not wear street shoes at home. They may declare that it is not necessary for foreign visitors to remove them, but will appreciate it when they do and will likely offer slippers.

Due to the rising incidence of crime, Russians are triple- and quadruple-locking their apartment doors, and they are reluctant to open them without knowing who is standing outside. To be sure they know who you are, call beforehand from a cell phone or nearby public phone and tell them you will be there shortly. Puzzling for Westerners is the Russian passion for *morozhenoye* (ice cream), which they consume outdoors even in the dead of winter with the temperature below freezing. Russian ice cream is very good, and the favorite flavor, as in the United States, is vanilla.

A greater passion, of course, is tea, the favorite nonalcoholic drink of Russians. On a per capita basis, Russia is second only to Great Britain in tea consumption, and half of all Russians are believed to drink at least five cups a day. Russians like their tea black and loose; tea bags are popular mainly with young businesspeople and students, for whom time is important. Traditionally, tea is brewed in a *samovar* (self-boiler), where the water is heated in a metal vessel with an inner cylinder filled with burning coals. Another novelty for foreign visitors may be the *podstakannik* (literally, an "underglass"), a metal glass holder with a handle on one side. Tea prepared and drunk in such a manner is a sight to see.

THE TOAST

Za vashe zdorovye *(To your health).*

—A short Russian toast

Visitors should be prepared to raise their glasses in a toast. Toasting in Russia is serious business, and in the Republic of Georgia it is an art form.

Toasts are usually made at the beginning of a meal when vodka is consumed with the first course, or at the end of the meal after the sweet wine or champagne that is served with dessert, and often throughout the meal as well. Hosts toast first, and the ranking guest is expected to follow with a return toast. With each toast, glasses are clinked with those of other guests while looking at each guest directly and making eye contact. The person being toasted also drinks.

In contrast to the laconic American or British "cheers" or "bottoms up," a toast in Russia is a short speech. For starters, there are the obligatory thanks to the hosts for their hospitality. This may be followed by references to the purpose of the visit, to international cooperation, peace and friendship, and the better world we hope to leave to our children as a result of our cooperation. Be poetic and dramatic when making a toast, and let your "soul" show. Russians appreciate a show of emotion and imagination. Make the most of your toast and don't hesitate to exaggerate. Humor may be used, but the substance of the toast should be serious. Russians will judge a toast as an indication of the seriousness of a visitor's purpose. Prudent travelers will have a few toasts prepared in advance; they will surely be needed.

Women, by tradition, do not toast in Russia, but more and more Russian women are now doing so, and Russians will not be surprised if a foreign woman raises her glass and gives a toast. And if a hostess is present, she gets a separate toast, complimenting her on her home, food, and hospitality, but never on her looks, as pretty as she may be.

In Georgia, which is now independent, toasting is continuous throughout the meal, and a guest's glass is never left empty. Eating, drinking, and hospitality are a way of life in Georgia, a wine-producing country, and guests should be prepared for meals that last several hours. Once, when I was in Georgia as the leader of an American delegation, my hosts had the courtesy to ask in advance whether I preferred a three- or four-hour dinner. I opted for the three-hour "short" dinner, which actually lasted five hours—with continuous eating, drinking, animated conversation, music, singing, and endless toasting. *Omnia pro patria.*

Mir i druzhba (peace and friendship) is a toast—as well as slogan—that visitors will often hear in Russia; so often, in fact, that it begins to sound more and more like the political catchphrase it once was throughout the communist bloc. Of the misuse of the word *peace,* Vaclav Havel, the Czech playwright who became his country's democratically elected president in 1990, has written:

> For forty years now I have read it on the front of every building and in every shop window in my country. For forty years, an allergy to that beautiful word has been engendered in me as in every one of my fellow citizens because I know what the word has meant here for the past forty years: ever mightier armies ostensibly to defend peace.[148]

Political slogans aside, the Russian yearning for peace and friendship should not be seen as an attempt to delude the West but as a reflection of their traditional yearning for harmony, cooperation, and community.

Russians have good reason to want peace and friendship with other countries, although that did not prevent their leaders from using armed force when they believed it necessary—in Hungary in 1956, Czechoslovakia in 1968, Afghanistan in 1979, and in Chechnya in their own country, as well.

The death and destruction of World War II is still a part of every Russian's life, experienced either directly or through older family members. More than 20 million Soviet citizens died in the war, and much of European Russia was overrun by German armies before their advance was halted and reversed at Stalingrad. Leningrad was besieged for 900 days, and more than a million of its people died there of hunger alone—more than 10 times the deaths at Hiroshima. The Great Patriotic War, as the Russians call it, was truly one of the epic events of Russian history, one that threatened the very existence of the state. More recently, another generation has known war, in Afghanistan and Chechnya.

Do Russians fear a war with the United States? Some of them may, because the U.S. is the only country with the military might to vanquish them. Russians, moreover, have a very high respect for American technology, military as well as civilian. When Russians toast "peace and friendship" with Americans, they really mean it.

ALCOHOL, THE OTHER "-ISM"

More people are drowned in a glass than in the ocean.

—Russian proverb

To all the other "-isms" that help one to understand Russians, alcoholism must unfortunately be added. For Karl Marx, religion was the opiate of the people. For Russians, the opiate has been alcohol.

The Russian affinity for alcohol was described by the Marquis de Custine in 1839:

> The greatest pleasure of these people is drunkenness; in other words, forgetfulness. Unfortunate beings! they must dream, if they would be happy. As proof of the good temper of the Russians, when the Muzhiks get tipsy, these men, brutalized as they are, become softened, instead of infuriated. Unlike the drunkards of our country, who quarrel and fight, they weep and embrace each other. Curious and interesting nation![149]

In our time, the distinguished Russian novelist and literary critic Andrei Sinyavsky has described drunkenness as

> . . . our *idée fixe*. The Russian people drink not from need and not from grief, but from an age-old requirement for the miraculous and the extraordinary—drink, if you will mystically, striving to transport the soul beyond earth's gravity and return it to its sacred noncorporeal state. Vodka is the Russian muzhik's White Magic; he decidedly prefers it to Black Magic—the female.[150]

Per capita consumption of alcohol in Russia and the United States is not very different. Americans, however, drink more wine and beer, Russians more hard liquor, mainly vodka. And like their North European neighbors from Ireland to Finland, Russians drink their distilled spirits "neat," without a mixer, and in one gulp.

Vodka is described by Hedrick Smith as "one of the indispensable lubricants and escape mechanisms of Russian life. . . . Russians drink to blot out the tedium of life, to warm themselves from the chilling winters, and they eagerly embrace the escapism it offers."[151]

To take the measure of a man, Russians will want to drink with him, and the drinking will be serious. Americans should not attempt to match their hosts in drinking. This is one competition Russians should be allowed to win, as they surely will.

Vodka is also a prelude to business transactions. As one Western financier explains:

> Business is done differently everywhere. In Russia . . . any negotiation is preceded by an arranged dinner that is extremely boozy. . . . You can't expect to go in there with a stiff upper lip and a pressed suit. It's a test. The trick is to play the game, but not get distracted by it.[152]

Vodka is drunk straight, ice-cold in small glasses in one "bottoms-up" gulp. At meals it is served with the *zakuski,* the tasty Russian cold meats, fish, and fresh and pickled vegetables—and caviar when affordable. Guests should bear in mind that the zakuski are only the first course, and that several other courses will follow. With each round of vodka there will be a toast, and the drinking and toasting will continue until the bottle—or bottles—are empty. Russian vodka bottles do not have replaceable caps because once a bottle is opened, it is soon emptied and there is no need for a cap.

What should a visitor do when confronted with vodka and the obligatory toasts at a dinner where the visitor is guest of honor? If the guest knows when to stop, then by all means drink and enjoy it. Guests who fear they will not know their limit can abstain, pleading doctor's orders or religious reasons. Or they can down their first drink and slowly nurse subsequent rounds through the evening. (And if you have had too much to drink, don't go out on the street alone at night!)

Russians prefer to drink while seated, and the stand-up cocktail party, a Western innovation, is consequently alien. Anyone invited to a Russian home should expect to be seated, fed a substantial repast, and drink during the meal. When invited to an American home, Russians will expect more than chips or cheese and crackers.

A night on the town usually consists of an evening with friends at a restaurant—eating, drinking, and dancing for several hours to very loud music. The eating will also be serious. Older Russians recall the difficult days when food was scarce, and they relish a good meal with many courses that can last several hours. Toward the end of the evening there may be a bloody brawl among the more serious drinkers, which ends only when the militsia arrives.

"Demon vodka," as the Russians call it, is the national vice. Excessive vodka consumption is a major cause of absenteeism, low productivity, industrial accidents, wife beating, divorce and other family problems, birth defects, and a declining longevity. Tens of thousands of Russians die each year of alcohol poisoning from bootleg alcohol or alcohol-based substitutes. Alcohol also plays a major role in road accidents, homicides, suicides, and violent crime. It is also a contributing factor to Russia's very high rate of deaths from fires—more than 17,000 deaths in 2006, more than 10 times rates typical of Western Europe and the United States—because intoxicated people inadvertently set or are unable to escape fires.[153]

With the economic, social, and physical ills that alcohol causes, it was not surprising that the first published decree after Gorbachev took office in 1985 signaled a state campaign against it. The intent was to limit consumption, but the immediate result was a sugar shortage because Russians purchased more sugar to increase their production of *samogon* (home brew). Consumption of products with alcoholic content also increased—industrial alcohol, jet fuel, insecticide, perfume, shoe polish, and toothpaste—thus creating additional shortages. Gorbachev's antialcohol campaign also resulted in a 10 to 20 percent reduction in tax revenues.[154] An admitted failure, the program was scrapped after three years. The antialcohol campaign, however, did have one virtue. At the peak of the campaign, violent crime dropped and life expectancy for men immediately increased, but these trends reversed when the campaign ended.

Alcohol continues to take its toll, contributing heavily to the mortality rate for Russian males who imbibe toxic samogon and other alcohol-based substances, although the number of such deaths has been declining due to the imposition of taxes on industrial alcohols.[155] Particularly alarming has been the spread of alcoholism among teenagers and children, which often leads to suicide.[156]

Of the alcohol consumed in Russia, one bottle in every three is believed to be made clandestinely.[157] Travelers to Russia should beware of alcohol that is sold in street kiosks at bargain-basement prices. That bottle with the authentic-looking label may not be genuine, and it may be bad for your health.

Vodka is a basic ingredient of Russian life and will not be easily eliminated. During the height of the antialcohol campaign, I attended several official lunches in Moscow where wine was the strongest drink served. But as a reminder of our own Prohibition days, bottles of vodka were passed under the table among the thirsty guests.

Vodka does have one virtue. While it can produce a hangover when drunk to excess, it seldom causes a headache or nausea. And with zakuski, in moderation, it is the ideal drink.

VRANYO, THE RUSSIAN FIB

Yes, the Russian is incapable of telling downright lies; but seems equally incapable of telling the truth. The intermediate phenomenon for which he feels the utmost love and tenderness resembles neither truth nor lozh *[lie]. It is* vranyo. *Like our native aspen, it pops up uninvited everywhere, choking other varieties; like the aspen it is no use for firewood or carpentry; and, again like the aspen, it is sometimes beautiful.*

—Leonid Andreyev, *Pan-Russian Vranyo*

Russians can fudge the facts, a national characteristic called *vranyo* (vranyoh, with the accent on the second syllable).[158] Dictionaries translate vranyo as "lies, fibs, nonsense, idle talk, twaddle," but like many Russian terms, it is really untranslatable. Americans might call it "tall talk" or "white lies," but "fib" perhaps comes closest because vranyo, as Russian writer Leonid Andreyev noted, is somewhere between the truth and a lie. Vranyo is indeed an art form, beautiful perhaps to Russians but annoying to Westerners and others who value the unvarnished truth.

In its most common form today, vranyo is an inability to face the facts, particularly when the facts do not reflect favorably on Russia. Tourist guides are masters of vranyo, as are Russians who represent their country abroad. When ideology or politics dictate a particular position, they are likely to evade, twist, or misstate facts in order to put the best possible spin on a potentially embarrassing situation. As Boris Fedorov, a former deputy prime minister of Russia has put it, "There are several layers of truth in Russia. Nothing is black or white, fortunately or unfortunately."[159]

Russians, however, do not consider vranyo to be dishonest, nor should foreign visitors. As Fyodor Dostoyevsky declared:

> Among our Russian intellectual classes the very existence of a non-liar is an impossibility, the reason being that in Russia even honest men can lie. . . . I am convinced that in other nations, for the great majority, it is only scoundrels who lie; they lie for practical advantage, that is, with directly criminal aims.[160]

And, as Dostoyevsky might have put it, if vranyo is not a crime, it should not be punished.

When using vranyo, Russians know that they are fibbing and expect that their interlocutors will also know. But it is considered bad manners to directly challenge the fibber, although it can be done with tact. As Hingley advises, the victim of vranyo should "convey subtly, almost telepathically, that he is aware of what is going on, that he appreciates the performance and does not despise his . . . host simply because the conditions of the latter's office obliged him to put it on."[161]

I put that advice to good use in Moscow once when I was a victim of vranyo. At a lunch given by the American ambassador, all the Russian guests had arrived on time but one, and he had called me the day before to confirm his attendance. After waiting 30 minutes, the ambassador asked me to call our tardy guest and inquire whether we could expect him. An unknown voice took my call and told me that our guest had just suffered a heart attack and could not attend the lunch. Surmising that the illness was diplomatic and that our guest had been instructed by higher-ups not to attend, I called again the next day and our delinquent guest himself answered the phone. After expressing my regrets about his failure to show, I congratulated him on his speedy recovery and wished him continued good health.

Vranyo can also be used at high levels of government. In August 1991, during the attempted Moscow coup, Westerners wondered why so many apparently healthy Russian leaders, including Mikhail Gorbachev, were said to be ill and unavailable, only to surface in a few days looking quite healthy.

In December 1994 the Russian military was accused of assisting rebels who were attempting to topple the government of Chechnya, the Muslim republic in the Caucasus that had declared independence from the Russian Federation. Moscow denied the accusation, and when Russian soldiers in Chechnya were captured by Chechen forces, Moscow officials, including Defense Minister Grachev, claimed the captured soldiers were mercenaries. But when the soldiers admitted on Chechen television that they were members of a Russian military unit sent secretly to Chechnya by the KGB, the Russian defense ministry was forced to concede that they were indeed Russian military personnel.

Vranyo can even show up at summit meetings. During their May 1995 Moscow summit meeting, President Yeltsin assured President Bill Clinton that "there are no military actions going on in Chechnya," adding that "the Interior Ministry is now simply confiscating weapons still in the hands of small rebel bands."[162] Shortly after Yeltsin spoke, the media reported that Russian helicopters were attacking Chechen villages, firing rockets into farmhouses.

When the Russian nuclear submarine *Kursk*, with a crew of 118, sank in August 2000, the Russian navy issued a series of misstatements that minimized the seriousness of the accident, were patently false, and raised false hopes among families of the victims.[163]

The navy initially reported the accident on Monday, August 14, saying it had taken place on Sunday; in fact, it had occurred on Saturday. The navy said the *Kursk* was crippled by "technical faults," and the crew had allowed it to glide to the sea bed; actually, it was destroyed by explosions on board, flooded quickly and sank, and most of the crew died within minutes. A navy spokesman said rescuers were in radio contact with the crew; in fact, there was no radio contact from the moment of the accident. The navy also said that the crew had immediately signaled it had shut down the nuclear reactor, but officials later said that the reactor had been closed down automatically; in fact, the navy had no information from those on board. Officials also denied that the sub was flooded, adding that there was no damage to the hull. The next day, Tuesday, August 15, the navy announced that the crew had signaled that there had been no deaths on board, and officially denied that there had been some deaths. One day later, Wednesday, August 16, a high-ranking navy officer said the crew was continuing to send signals by tapping on the hull, and officials later announced that the last sound from the vessel had come on Monday. Finally, on Saturday, August 19, the navy acknowledged that damage to the sub had been massive, most of the crew had died within minutes, and the others were certainly dead.

Related to vranyo is *pokazukha,* the tradition of staging an event "for show," especially for high officials and visiting foreign dignitaries. The classic example is the "Potemkin village," named after one of Empress Catherine the Great's favorites. According to legend, false village facades were constructed along her travel route to show the empress how well her people were living. Pokazukha was continued in the Soviet era when life was portrayed as the government wanted it to be seen, not as it actually was. The Soviets, for example, staged the opening of the Baikal-Amur Railway in 1984, the target year for its completion, although the huge project was far from finished at the time.

If Russians are compelled by tradition to show only the best, Americans seem obliged to show the worst. As one Russian reported after visiting the United States, everywhere he went his American hosts showed him what was wrong, but also what was being done to correct it. By showing what is wrong, Americans are reflecting their optimism about being able to change things for the better. Russians, by showing the best, are revealing their embarrassment about shortcomings in their country, their inability to deal with them openly, and their pessimism for the future.

At times Russians may say something that an American finds patently wrong or unacceptable. Some Americans, preferring to avoid a confrontation, will choose to let it pass. But remaining silent in such a situation may create an impression of acquiescence that would be misleading. Depending on the importance of the issue under discussion, it may be preferable to point out the error even if it should lead to controversy. Russians respect persons who are candid and straightforward. If your facts are accurate, Russians will not be offended by being corrected. They will also not hesitate to correct an American, and their criticism should be accepted in the same spirit. This is a trait Russians and Americans share.

NYEKULTURNO

Instruction shapes your mind; upbringing, your manners.

—Russian proverb

Many an American has confidently entered a Russian theater or restaurant, outercoat draped over an arm as in the United States, only to be stopped by an usher or waiter and told to first check the coat.

Coats and other outerwear must be checked on entering office buildings, theaters, concert halls, restaurants, museums, and other public buildings. In the lobbies of those buildings visitors will find a *garderob* (cloakroom) staffed by one or more of those ubiquitous Russian grandmothers. The checking procedure is efficient and dependable, and tipping is not customary. Since people must bundle up in cold weather, the mandatory checking of outergarments makes good sense. But be sure that your coat has a loop sewn into it for hanging or you will be berated by the guardians of the garderob.

Everyday Russian life is full of other do's and don'ts, reflecting the state's efforts to impose new patterns of behavior on a newly urbanized citizenry only recently removed from their tradition-bound villages. There is a right way and a wrong way to do almost everything, and Russians will not hesitate to tell you when you are doing something wrong. The wrong way is termed *nyekulturno* (uncultured, bad manners, or vulgar), and a foreign visitor's behavior will be judged by the same standards.

Wearing coats in public buildings is nyekulturno, although Russians see nothing wrong in strolling through hotel corridors clad only in pajamas or bathrobes as if the hotel were a large communal apartment. Also nyekulturno are standing with hands in pants pockets, sprawling in chairs, placing feet on tables, crossing legs while seated so as to show the sole of a shoe, sitting with legs spread wide, crossing arms behind the head, draping an arm over the back of a chair, or merely lounging, all of which Americans are wont to do at times. An American student recalls being berated in Moscow for lounging on the steps of a public building as he might have done back home. People are expected to behave in public with a degree of decorum. These are not exclusively Russian attitudes; disdain for such demeanor may be found in many other European countries as well.

Many other liberties that Americans take for granted are also nyekulturno. Students do not eat, drink, or chew gum during class. Eating lunch on park lawns in the city is unacceptable. In the evening, theater patrons are expected to dress appropriately for opera, theater, and the symphony. When going into a theater aisle to reach your seat, turn facing the seated people you will be passing, rather than showing them your backside. Loud talk in public and being "pushy" are taboo; the quiet "sell" and modesty will get you further. Telling Russians that you have to go to the restroom is also nyekulturno. Simply excuse yourself; they'll know where you are going.

Russian performers, public speakers, and others on stage will join their audiences in applause, a move that puzzles Americans. They are, however, not applauding their own performance but are expressing approval and appreciation of the spectators and their response to the performance.

And I have had to explain to high-ranking American officials that whistling in a concert hall after a performance is not a sign of approval as in the United States; rather, it is a sign of disapproval in Russia (and elsewhere in Europe).

TIME AND PATIENCE

Punctuality has been exceedingly difficult to instill into a population unused to regular hours.

—Margaret Mead, *Soviet Attitudes Toward Authority*

Time is money to Americans, and punctuality is a virtue. Meetings are expected to start on time, and work under pressure of the clock is a challenge routinely accepted. To Russians, however, with their agricultural heritage, time is like the seasons—a time to reap and a time to sow, and a time for doing little in between.

Seychas budyit (it will be done right away) is an expression heard often in Russia, from waiters in restaurants, clerks in stores, and officials in offices. Be assured, however, that whatever has been promised will not be done right away but will more likely take some time.

Communism reinforced the native Russian disrespect for time, since workers could not be fired and there was no incentive to do things on time. Moreover, in a country where time is not a vital commodity, people become more sanguine about accepting delays. When something very important must be done, it will be done, and time and cost will not be obstacles. But time for Russians is not yet an economic commodity to be measured in rubles or dollars.

Being on time is consequently alien. Russians are notoriously late, and they think nothing of arriving long after the appointed hour, which is not considered as being late. (Concerts and theater performances, however, do start on time, and latecomers will not be seated until the first intermission.)

When Russians do arrive, there are a number of rituals that must be played out before the business part of a meeting can start. First, the small talk, a necessary part of all personal encounters; then, the customary tea or other drink, followed perhaps by talk about family and personal problems; and finally, the business of the day. All this takes time and usually does not start before ten o'clock in the morning.

The business part of the talk will also be lengthy, because important issues are approached in a roundabout rather than in a direct manner. Impatient foreign businesspeople will wonder when the key issues of the meeting will be discussed. And after the meeting has concluded and the visitor believes he has agreement to proceed, nothing may happen for weeks, or months, or ever.

For Russians, time is not measured in minutes or hours but more likely in days, weeks, and months. The venerated virtue is not punctuality but patience. As a student from India who had spent four years in Moscow advised me, "Be patient, hope for the best, but prepare for the worst. Everything here takes time, and sometimes never gets done."

Americans and many other nationalities are oriented toward doing; Russians, toward contemplating. As a Russian psychiatrist explained to me, "Russians can look at an object all day and reflect on it but take no action." When faced with an issue to be resolved, they will first think through the historical, philosophical, and ideological considerations as well as the consequences of whatever is to be decided. In contrast, Americans and other "doers" will first consider the practical points, the obstacles to be overcome, the details, and how to get from here to there.

A Russian conference interpreter, recalling her experience with Russians and Americans in the evenings after their formal meetings had adjourned, told me, "The Russians would sit all night drinking tea, discussing and reflecting, while the Americans would be thinking about what they had to do the next day and preparing to do it."

Such divergent views of time can create difficulties in cooperative efforts and joint ventures. Americans will want to negotiate an agreement expeditiously, schedule an early start on the venture, begin on time, meet production deadlines, complete the work as promptly as possible, and show early results or profit. Russians will need more time to get organized, and there will be frequent delays and postponements. They will be less concerned with immediate results, and profit is a concept that they are just now beginning to understand. The job may be completed, but only after considerable prodding from the American side.

What to do? Not much, except to persist patiently, and speak softly but carry a big prod. Once prodded and made to understand that a deadline must be met, Russians can show prodigious bursts of energy and will work around the clock to complete the job.

THE RUSSIAN LANGUAGE

The Russian language surpasses all European languages, since it has the magnificence of Spanish, the liveliness of French, the strength of German, the delicacy of Italian, as well as the richness and conciseness of Greek and Latin.

—M. V. Lomonosov

Foreigners most successful in understanding the Russians, as readers will have noted by now, are those who speak some Russian. Speakers of Russian— be they businesspeople, journalists, scholars and scientists, professional or citizen diplomats—have a significant advantage. Communication may be possible with smiles, hand signals, body language, and interpreters, but the ability to carry on a conversation in Russian raises the relationship to a more meaningful level.

Those who are put off by the challenge of studying Russian should know that it is far easier to learn than many other languages such as Chinese, Arabic, or Finnish. Russians, moreover, are not offended by foreigners with an inadequate command of Russian. Many of their own citizens also speak Russian poorly.

The study of Russian in the United States has declined significantly since the end of the Cold War. In 1993, some 14,700 students were enrolled in precollege study of Russian, but by 2007 there were only an estimated 8,000 to 10,000.[164] In 1990 there were 44,626 college students studying Russian, but by 2006 this had decreased to 24,848.[165] As Russians have often pointed out, there are more teachers of English in the Soviet Union (about 100,000) than students of Russian in the U.S.

How to explain this? There is some speculation that the decline in Russian language study is an element of the "peace dividend." As possibilities for

U.S.-Russian conflict decline, so does interest in Russian language study in the United States. That defies logic, of course, since reform in Russia and the improvement in U.S.-Russian relations open up many opportunities for Americans to interact with Russians.

But the study of Russian in the CIS and the three Baltic states has also declined, a development that Russian Foreign Minister Sergei Lavrov described as "alarming," adding that "the strengthening of the positions of the Russian language and Russian culture in the world is one of the main tasks for Russia."[166]

Russian is a Slavic language, as are Ukrainian, Belarusian, Polish, Czech, Slovak, Bulgarian, and several other related tongues. They are all Indo-European languages, a group that includes, among others, the Germanic, Romance, and English languages, all of which have common roots.

Russian and English have common roots? While this at first may seem difficult to imagine, Russian and English do have many cognates—related words with a common root. That most basic word *milk,* for example, is a cognate to the German *milch,* Polish *mleko,* and Russian *moloko.* Compare also *apple* with the German *apfel,* Polish *jablko* (pronounced "yablkoh"), and Russian *yabloko.* Notice also that the words become longer, adding a syllable or two as they travel east from English and German to Polish and Russian. Perhaps this is why English has so many four-letter words.

It takes about 10 to 15 percent longer to say something in Russian than in English, and experienced translators say that they will often need three or more Russian words for one English word. Add to this the Russian tendency to be long-winded—a characteristic of agricultural societies, the old American South included—and you have another reason for Russian verbosity.

Another difficulty with Russian results from the shifting accentuation of words. There is no general rule on where the stress falls in a word or sentence, as there is in most European languages, but a Russian word placed at the beginning of a sentence will have more importance than when placed at the end.

The Cyrillic alphabet, named after St. Cyril, the apostle to the Slavs who devised the Glagolitic alphabet on which Cyrillic is based, may also faze some students. Russian, however, is mostly pronounced as it is written. If you can read Cyrillic, you can pronounce it. This makes Russian pronunciation easier than English, where words are seldom pronounced as they are written.

Foreigners who do not speak Russian should at least learn the alphabet before traveling to Russia. Knowing the thirty-two letters of the Cyrillic alphabet will enable travelers to read signs, menus, and the names of Metro stations and will considerably facilitate a stay. It will also give visitors a start in building a Russian vocabulary. A basic vocabulary can be easily acquired by learning a few root words and the Russian equivalents of English prefixes, suffixes, and prepositions. Moreover, many of those long and imposing Russian words are structured exactly as their Western equivalents are.

Russian has acquired numerous words from Western languages. Many mechanical, medical, and technical terms are from German; artistic and cultural words from French; and business and modern scientific terms from English. More recently, many English words previously unknown in Russia have also come into common usage—*kserokopiya* (Xerox copy), *faks* (fax), *mikser* (mixer), *forvardy* (forward), *optsiony* (options), *dzhinsy* (jeans), *keeleri* (contract killers), and *biznesmeni* (businessmen)—although they are given a Russian pronunciation and often a Slavic ending.

Words are inflected, as in Latin and German, to denote such distinctions as case, gender, number, tense, person, and mood. And Russian verbs have two aspects—the imperfective for repeated actions and the perfective for completed actions. Ronald Hingley wonders, facetiously, whether it is not this strict separation of these two aspects of the verb that makes it so difficult for Russians to complete actions.[167] The grammar sounds complex, and it is, but there are a few rules that explain it all. Although Russian can be learned cold, it helps to know another inflected European language.

Russian is also replete with negatives, and positive ideas are often expressed negatively. An object will be "not big" rather than "small." A Russian will describe his or her feelings as "not bad" rather than "good." And a double negative in Russian does not make an affirmative as in English; instead, it emphasizes the negative. The more negatives in a sentence, the more negative the meaning.

Younger Russians with access to computers are starting to use the universal Internet language. This is a development that bothers the "purists," much as the introduction of anglicisms in France bothered the French Academy in the years following World War II. To protect against what they see as an assault on the Russian language, the government declared 2007 as the "Year of the Russian Language in Russia and the World," and it has taken steps to promote the study of Russian abroad.

One final caveat—while Russian has its share of earthy and vulgar expressions, they are not used in polite society.

MISUNDERSTANDINGS

There are two ways you can tell when a man is lying. One is when he says he can drink champagne all night and not get drunk. The other is when he says he understands Russians.

—Charles E. Bohlen, former U.S. ambassador to Moscow

Russian is a very rich language. In English one word may suffice to convey an idea, while Russian will have several words to choose from, each with a slightly different shade of meaning. This presents problems for interpreters and translators, as well as possibilities for misunderstandings.

Many words and expressions in one language simply do not exist in the other. Aleksei Mikhalev, a Russian translator of American literature, says that differences in language and literature—two significant products of a nation's thought and psychology—demonstrate that English speakers and Russians are not very much alike. He cites the impossibility of finding precise Russian equivalents for the simple English word *privacy,* a concept that does not exist in Russian (nor in many other languages as well). Other untranslatables from English to Russian listed by Mikhalev include *take care, have fun, make love, efficiency,* and *challenge.*[168]

Even translatable words are sometimes mistranslated, especially when idiomatic language is involved. Kornei Chukovsky, one of the best-known translators from English into Russian, cited several such bloopers. In one, an experienced Russian translator, translating a work by American poet Langston Hughes, wrote about the passionate love of a black man for a black woman who had rejected him. Actually, Hughes had written about a "black maria" (police van) that he hoped was not coming to get him. Another example cited by Chukovsky, from Galsworthy's *The Forsyte Saga,* had a young man, Michael Mont, rowing a boat with his girlfriend across a river when he suddenly "caught a crab" (a rowing term indicating a faulty stroke). The Russian translator had Mont fishing for crabs in the middle of an ardent conversation with his sweetheart.[169]

A seemingly simple expression can have one meaning in English and another in Russian, as I learned when helping to arrange the first loan between a Russian and American museum. In 1973, the National Gallery of Art in Washington, D.C., sought to borrow a painting by Rembrandt from Moscow's Pushkin Museum. In the spirit of detente, the Soviet government agreed to lend the work, but it first sought assurance that the U.S.

government would guarantee the security of the valuable Rembrandt while it was in the United States.

In response to an official request for a guarantee, I informed the Soviet cultural attaché that the State Department would take "all possible measures" to safeguard the Rembrandt. That was boilerplate language used to indicate that the department would do all it possibly could—in this case merely requesting the museum and local authorities to take appropriate measures to protect the painting. The Soviet diplomat then asked, in Russian, whether that meant *vsyo vozmozhnoye* (everything possible), an expression that is much stronger in Russian than in English, with the emphasis on "everything." I repeated, in English, that the State Department would take all possible measures. My Russian colleague accepted that as vsyo vozmozhnoye, which satisfied Moscow's needs. Had the Rembrandt been damaged or stolen, it might have been the end of his career—and mine.

To prevent misunderstandings, anyone planning to give an oral presentation to Russians should also present a paper with the principle points. A written statement will help to avoid the hazards of interpreting, as well as the tendency of Russians to think in general rather than specific terms. Presenting a paper also ensures that Russians will know exactly what the visitor intended to say, regardless of what was actually said and how it was translated into Russian.

COMMUNICATION DIFFERENCES

Russia has an oral rather than a written tradition—understandable in a country where most of the people were illiterate until less than a century ago—and talking comes naturally to its people. Every Russian seems to be a born orator. Conversations begin easily between complete strangers as well as between men and women. The complexities of the language notwithstanding, it can be a pleasure to listen to Russian speech. Delivery is unhurried, often eloquent, and without pretense. But Russians can also talk around a difficult issue without addressing it directly. Listeners should pay close attention to what is left unsaid in addition to what is said. As Lyudmila Putin, wife of the former president, once told a German friend, "You must always listen between the words and read between the lines."[170]

Don't expect short responses to simple questions. The question-and-answer approach simply will not do. Rather than respond with a brief yes or no, Russians are more likely to give a lengthy explanation that will leave the listener wondering whether the answer is indeed yes or no. Former *Washington Post* correspondent David Remnick recalls how, in an interview with Mikhail Gorbachev, "I asked a question, and he finished his answer forty minutes later. . . ."[171]

Body language is important. Russians use hands and facial expressions to express ideas and emotions, in contrast to Anglo-Saxons who consider such demeanor distracting if not unmannerly. Through body language, a person's intent can be determined without even understanding the words. Facial expressions are also clues to behavior. Americans are taught to open conversations with a smile and to keep smiling. Russians tend to start out with grim faces, but when they do smile, it reflects relaxation and progress in developing a good relationship. Winks and nods are also good signs, but if a stony look continues, you are not getting through and are in trouble.

Physical contact by Russians—touching another person—is a sign that things are going well and that a degree of rapport has been reached. The degree of physical contact will indicate how well things are going. Placing a hand on another person's arm, for example, or embracing, are good signs.

Closeness and physical contact with other persons are much more common in Russia than in the West, a heritage of the village past when people lived in close proximity in small huts. Russians also stand very close when conversing, often less than twelve inches, which is closer than most Americans will find comfortable. They gesticulate more and do not hesitate to make physical contact and invade the other person's space.

An American teacher of Russian recalls how, while studying at Moscow State University, a Russian instructor playfully rapped the knuckles of some Americans in his class as a sign of displeasure over their inadequate preparation for the day's lesson:

> The American men, in an uproar at both the teacher's invasion of their space and his use of body contact to enforce his wishes, went immediately after class to the director to complain about the instructor's behavior. . . . As a result, the instructor was reprimanded and told to maintain "a proper distance" from his students and to refrain from all physical contact with Americans, "who do not understand these things."[172]

There are times, however, when Russian knuckles should be rapped. "The Russian is never more agreeable than after his knuckles have been sharply rapped," wrote George F. Kennan. "He takes well to rough play and rarely holds grudges over it."[173]

Straight talk is appreciated, even when it leads to disagreement. But when disagreement does occur, Russians appreciate honesty rather than attempts to paper over differences. It is far better to level with them and to be certain that they fully understand your position. They respect adversaries who are straightforward and sincere in expressing views that diverge from their own.

Former Secretary of State Colin Powell, en route to a meeting with Russian Foreign Minister Igor S. Ivanov, recalled his long record of interactions with Russian leaders over the years as national security adviser and chairman of the Joint Chiefs of Staff in the first Bush administration. "If one speaks openly and candidly," said Powell, "you can make progress as long as you don't shy away from the tough issues and as long as you don't forget that there are many areas of interest that we have in common."[174]

But confrontations over differences of views can often be avoided by letting Russians talk themselves out. After they have expressed their righteousness and indignation and have unburdened themselves, their opposition may moderate and the differences may turn out to be less than originally believed. In fact, after talking themselves out, Russians and Americans may even find that they have a unanimity of views.

Nyet is a simple Russian word that is often misunderstood, and it seems to be an almost automatic response by Russians when asked if something can be done. Clerks, doormen, officials, and others seem to prefer the easy response, "Nyet."

There can be several reasons for the automatic nyet. One common explanation is "We don't do it that way here." Or the item requested in a store or restaurant may not be available. Or the clerk may not care whether it is available, or may not be at all interested in helping the customer. In any event, Russians do not routinely accept a nyet, and neither should you. Continue talking, keep your cool, don't raise your voice, smile, and keep repeating your request. As noted before, a good interpersonal relationship can often overcome the obstacle, whatever it may be, and beat the system.

A nyet, however, when expressed in a manner indicating that the real response is "perhaps," may indicate that a little incentive is needed. In such cases, a few dollars discreetly brought into view may produce the desired effect.

THE TELEPHONE

Telephones in Russia are enough to make the most patient man curse.
—Irving R. Levine, Main Street, U.S.S.R.

Irving R. Levine was NBC correspondent in Moscow in the 1950s, but his description of the Russian telephone system may still be valid in many parts of the country. Service in Moscow, St. Petersburg, and a few other large cities is good and comparable to the West, but in smaller cities and rural areas the service is inadequate, the technology ancient, and the cursing continues.

The Russian telephone system underwent significant changes in the 1990s as it made progress toward building the telecommunications infrastructure necessary for a market economy. More than 1,000 companies are now licensed to offer communication services, access to digital lines has improved in urban centers, Internet and e-mail services are available, and there are cybercafes in major cities. However, a large demand for telephone service remains unsatisfied, and in many cities there is a long wait to have a home phone installed.

Despite the advances in technology, a culture that values personal relations prefers to communicate face-to-face, and doing business from a distance can therefore be difficult. Russians relate well to people but not through letters or telephones, another legacy of the oral tradition and life in the village. Letters are answered late, if at all. Fax and e-mail may get a better response, but that is by no means assured. So what happens when you try to use the telephone, the preferred medium for communication in the West?

First, know the number you're calling. For many years there was no Moscow telephone directory. One was eventually published in 1990, but only 250,000 copies were printed—hardly enough for a city of more than 10 million. Now directories are published for business and government phones, and there are Yellow Pages in English. Directories are also available on the Internet, but before departing for Moscow it is advisable to obtain from earlier travelers the numbers of people you will be trying to reach. And when in Moscow, a "little black book" will be useful for recording the numbers of people you may want to contact later. Public phones that work with a telephone card are also available. Cards may be purchased at Metro stations and other sites, and can be used to call anywhere in Russia or the world. Cell phones are common in Moscow and other large cities.

On the phone, Russians may seem abrupt or noncommittal. They are not accustomed to doing business by phone because the service may be bad or they suspect that their phone may be bugged. If you are able to agree on a time and place for a meeting, your call will have been a success. It may also come as a surprise to learn that many Russian officials do not mind being called at home. In fact, many of them have their office and home phone numbers on their vizitnaya card.

One Soviet writer's surprise reaction to how Americans use the telephone tells us as much about Russia as about the United States. After visiting the U.S., he wrote:

> One rarely hears of business meetings in the United States. All matters are settled straightaway on the spot, by telephone. Whichever establishment you call you may be sure that the man you want will be available. If, for some important reason, he's not there, a secretary will answer and will always tell you affably and politely who can help you instead, or will tell you exactly when the person you need will be back and when you should call him. The most complex questions are settled by telephone.[175]

RUSSIANS AND AMERICANS

You Russians and we Americans! Our countries so distant, so unlike at first glance—such a difference in social and political conditions, and our respective methods of moral and practical development the last hundred years— and yet in certain features, and vastest ones, so resembling each other.

—Walt Whitman, *Letter to a Russian*

Despite Russia's ambivalence toward the West, and notwithstanding the political and cultural differences and the often diametrically opposed values of the two societies, most Russians like Americans.

"The foreign country in which the majority of Russians . . . are most interested is America," wrote Sir William Hayter, a former British ambassador to Moscow. "It is the goal they are constantly being urged, or urging themselves, to 'catch up and overtake.' They share many tastes with it—love of gadgets, technology, massive scale. . . . America is their favorite foreign country."[176]

During my own service in Moscow with the American Embassy at the height of the Vietnam War, I never once met a Russian who held anything against me as an American. How could that be, given our differences then and the steady stream of anti-American propaganda that Russians were fed in their media over so many decades?

To begin with, the effect of anti-American propaganda should be discounted. Until glasnost, few Russians believed what their media told them.

If news was official, it was doubted; if a rumor, it was believed. Russians have had good reason to question official pronouncements.

In a country whose thousand-year history records one war after another—and with immense suffering—Russians know that they have never had a war with the United States. They also know that Russians and Americans were allies against their most recent enemy, Germany, in two world wars. Moreover, there are no territorial disputes between the two countries, a common cause of conflict.

Russia and the United States have no trade rivalries, nor do they compete in world markets. Many Russians also recall the aid they received from the United States—in the famine of the 1920s, the industrialization of the 1920s and 1930s, and the Lend-Lease of the 1940s during the darkest days of their life-and-death struggle with Nazi Germany. Indeed, some Soviet military vehicles were commonly known in Russian as "Willys" and "Studebakers" because the first jeeps and trucks to arrive from the U.S. during the war bore the names of those companies.

Fascination with machinery is shared by Russians and Americans. The best way to start a conversation with Russians, as I learned in Moscow, was to open the hood of my American station wagon on a downtown street and start tinkering with the engine. Immediately, I would be surrounded by a crowd asking how many "horses" the engine had, how fast the car could go, how much gas it used (in liters per hundred kilometers), and how much it cost.

But to go beyond casual conversation and really get to know Russians, you must sit down with them and eat and drink together. The best conversations with Russians occur, as earlier noted, at the kitchen table. The highlight of a visit to the United States by a delegation of senior Russian officials occurred when they sat around a kitchen table with American farmers in the Midwest and discussed farming far into the night.

I had a similar experience once when I dropped in unannounced at the library of the Siberian Academy of Sciences in Novosibirsk. Identifying myself as the cultural counselor of the American Embassy, I asked to see the library director. Surprised by the unexpected visit of an American diplomat, he graciously ushered me into his office. The legendary Russian hospitality soon showed itself when he sent an assistant out to get something for us to eat. She returned shortly with a long spicy sausage, a loaf of good black bread, a bottle of vodka, and an old kitchen knife, and our conversation warmed with our stomachs as we sat at his desk eating and drinking—without plates, forks, or napkins—and discussing libraries and book exchanges between our two countries. (His main complaint was that most of the books that the country received from abroad stayed in Moscow and did not reach Siberia.)

America's power and size also attract Russians—the "big is beautiful" syndrome. Russians see themselves and Americans as citizens of two great powers destined to play leading roles on the world stage. As a Russian professor explained to me, "We have more in common with Americans than with West Europeans. Both our countries have no aristocracies, both are big and without the complexes of small nations."

Joint endeavors between Russians and Americans are therefore seen as natural. Indeed, Russians get a psychological lift from working with Americans, regarding such cooperation as recognition of their coequal status. But they also expect Americans to accept them as equals, to return their admiration, and they are disappointed and puzzled when we do not.

One standard Russian complaint against Americans, writes Eliza K. Klose, is that they lack *dusha,* or soul:

> Many [in the former Soviet Union] believe that for all their welcoming smiles and quick friendliness, Americans are too preoccupied with earning a living to make the kind of long-term commitments to others that people in the former Soviet Union equate with friendship and cultural depth.[177]

Americans may indeed lack soul, but Russians nevertheless are very curious about the United States, and there is no country they wish to visit more. Many exciting innovations in their lives have come from America—jazz, jeans, Coke and Pepsi, and Big Macs, to name a few. Russians who were able to visit the U.S. during the Soviet years were astounded by the abundance they found there and the high standard of living. On seeing their first American supermarket, many believed it to be a "Potemkin village," a setup created to impress foreigners. Others, confused by the choices offered to consumers, questioned the need for so many different brands of the same product.

Russians recognize that most Americans may be far richer than they are, but they resent being talked down to. While Russians themselves are outspokenly critical of their own society, they can be hypersensitive to criticism by a foreigner. As one Russian teacher told me, "We think of America as the rich cousin who has material wealth, meeting Russia, the poor cousin, who has spiritual wealth. We are envious of your material wealth, but don't flaunt it. We know you have it."

But much of what Russians see in the United States confuses them. Puzzling are the free choices Americans have, the seeming lack of order, the concern for individual rights, the decay of our great cities, and the decentralization of the economy. Indeed, some Russians, after touring the U.S., have been certain that there must be some secret center that controls and runs the economy. How else could it perform so well?

To Americans, Russians are also puzzling. Why is it so difficult and time-consuming to reach agreement with them? Why do they always seem to be delaying decisions instead of being reasonable and meeting us halfway? Why are they so mistrustful of others, and can they be trusted to honor agreements? Despite some similarities, Russians and Americans are indeed different, Walt Whitman's words notwithstanding. Familiarization with the differences is the first step to bridging them.

But familiarity can also breed contempt. Criticism of the West, and the United States in particular, is now heard across the Russian political spectrum but mainly among the intellectuals and political elite, some of whom believe that the U.S. deliberately set about to destroy the Soviet Union, first through Mikhail Gorbachev and then through Boris Yeltsin. Others blame the U.S. for the dislocations caused by the collapse of communism, the precipitous decline of social services, the rapid deterioration of public health, and the sharp increases in crime, violence, and corruption.

Many Russians also resent the large influx of Americans and other Westerners who have descended on Moscow and give it the appearance of a boomtown. Foreigners no longer live in isolated enclaves, nor do they shop in exclusive hard-currency-only supermarkets where a wide range of Western products could be purchased. All goods in Russia must now be sold for rubles, and Western products are available to all in stores across Moscow and other major cities, although often at prices beyond the reach of most Russians. But the range and quality of the products displayed have made many Russians resentful of foreigners, as well as the small class of Russian businesspeople and mafia who flaunt their own affluence and high lifestyles.

SIX

Negotiating with Russians

If there are found among the Russians, better diplomatists than among other nations . . . it is because our journals inform them of every thing which is done or projected among ourselves, and because instead of prudently disguising our weaknesses, we display them, with passion, every morning; whilst, on the contrary, the Byzantine policy of the Russians, working in the dark, carefully conceals from us everything that is thought, done, or feared among them. We march exposed on all sides, they advance under cover. The ignorance in which they leave us blinds our view; our sincerity enlightens theirs; we suffer from all the evils of idle talking, they have all the advantages of secrecy; and herein lies all their skill and ability. . .

—Marquis de Custine, *Empire of the Czar*

THE ART OF NEGOTIATION

Don't hurry to reply, but hurry to listen.

—Russian proverb

Negotiation is an art well known to diplomats, lawyers, and business executives. Two parties meet, each with its own objectives, and attempt to reach a mutually acceptable agreement that will satisfy their basic needs. The goal for each side is to gain as much as possible while giving up only what is necessary to reach an agreement. At this age-old game the Russians are experts, in part because they are not in a hurry.

Where the two sides have similar goals, as is often the case when negotiations are entered into willingly, the process can be relatively easy. Both sides seek to reach agreement and have hopes of doing so; otherwise, they would not have agreed to meet. But when Russians and Americans negotiate, there are often considerations that may make it difficult to agree.

For the United States and Russia, the negotiation of minor issues may be amplified out of proportion because of their rivalry, thereby making minor issues appear more important than they really are. Agreement in principle on broad objectives may be easy to reach, but how the agreement will be carried out—the details of implementation—are usually more difficult. Long-standing policy may have to be modified by one side or the other. The terms of the agreement must satisfy the legal, political, and ideological requirements of both sides—yes, Americans may also have ideological considerations. And the subject under negotiation may be related to other issues for which one side or the other may not wish to establish a precedent.

Most Americans who negotiate with Russians represent only themselves or their organizations, while the Russians in negotiations may represent their government or need government approval before signing. Russian negotiators, moreover, are likely to be under strict instructions and without the flexibility of their American opposites to make on-the-spot decisions. When the negotiators represent private entities, they will have more flexibility.

The greatest challenge, however, results from the different Russian and American approaches to negotiations. Americans generally regard compromise as desirable and inevitable, a logical way of conducting business—meet them halfway and make a deal. Americans, consequently, regard any inability to reach agreement easily and quickly as failure. Russians regard compromise as a sign of weakness, a retreat from a correct and morally justified position. Russians, therefore, are great "sitters," prepared to wait out their opposite numbers in the expectation that time and Russian patience will produce more concessions from the impatient Americans. Soviet Foreign Minister Vyacheslav Molotov was dubbed "Stonebottom" because of his ability to outsit the Americans.

Chess is a Russian national pastime, and Russians negotiate in the same way they play chess, planning several moves ahead. Americans should think through the consequences of each move before making it, since it may establish a precedent that the Russians will cite later on, or it may lead to a tack in the negotiations different from the one expected.

Russian negotiating teams are usually composed of veterans who negotiate year-round with representatives of other countries. Americans, products of a mobile society, are more likely to be new to their positions and less experienced in the art of negotiation, particularly with Russians.

A concept or word from one side of the table may not be understood by the other because it simply does not exist in the other side's politics, laws, culture, or even language. Add to this the limitations of what Americans and Russians know and understand about each other, and the task of negotiating with the Russians becomes even more challenging.

Equality, reciprocity, and mutual advantage are watchwords that need to be kept in mind. Russians and Americans negotiate as equals, and Russians are very sensitive to any intimations that they are not being treated with sufficient respect and dignity. Agreements reached should provide for reciprocity—what is done in one country should be matched by a similar action in the other, and under conditions as equal as possible. And most important, the benefits to each side should be comparable.

Negotiations can be lengthy, tedious, and demanding. Negotiation, however, is the only way to do business with Russians—a handshake alone will not do—and Americans should understand the basic rules of the game before entering the playing field.

PROCEDURES AND TACTICS

Where there is sense, there is order.

—Russian proverb

The first step in any negotiation is to know what you want. That may sound overly simple, but often it is not. Many negotiators go into meetings without knowing precisely what their objectives are. Americans had better think through their objectives and define them clearly, because the Russians will certainly know their own.

Next, draft the text of an agreement that includes all your objectives. This is your maximum position—what you ideally would like to see in the final document. The Russians will also have their draft with their objectives, and it will represent their maximum position. Each side should understand that this is merely the opening bid—as in an Eastern bazaar—and neither should expect the other to accept the initial draft it has placed on the table. To save time, drafts may be exchanged in advance of the actual negotiations so that each side may study the other's objectives and draft language and be better prepared to negotiate.

Russian negotiating strategy reflects differences in thought patterns between East and West. Western negotiators prefer a pragmatic and detailed approach, discussing one issue at a time and progressing systematically toward a final agreement. Russians prefer a more general and conceptual approach, without specificity.

In political negotiations, for example, Russians will often seek agreement "in principle," which will be in harmony with an ideological framework or universal outlook. Such an agreement, which provides greater flexibility when the time for implementation arrives, will include high-sounding ideals couched in lofty language but few details. Americans should start with simple proposals and develop the complexities later, but not so late that they may be considered by the Russians to be of insufficient importance to be taken seriously. If numbers are important, they should be specified and their importance emphasized. Russians tend to be inexact when it comes to numbers. In commercial negotiations, however, or where money is involved, Russians will be sticklers for detail, insisting on a more detailed contract than is usual in international business.

The protocol of who sits where at the negotiating table should be observed. The Russian head of delegation may sit at the center of the table, flanked on both sides by an interpreter and aides in descending order of rank. Or the chairperson may sit at the head of the table. Whatever the arrangement, Americans should match it, with their chairperson seated across from his or her Russian opposite number. The two chairpersons should be of comparable rank, and a high-ranking visitor will be taken more seriously.

In their opening statement, Russians will provide a philosophical or ideological basis for their negotiating position. The opening statement may also provide clues to specific positions they will take later on and reveal previously unstated objectives or difficulties that were not anticipated.

In the give-and-take of negotiations, Russians will attempt to size up their opposite number. Who is this person? Is he or she serious, strong, and trustworthy? In making this assessment, Russians, like boxers, will bob and weave, feint and probe for weaknesses, and press forward vigorously when they sense a willingness to accommodate their views. When a probe meets with resistance, they will pull back and regroup.

Russian delivery style can be dramatic and emotional, intended to demonstrate true commitment to the position being espoused. Tough talk may also be used to beat down adversaries. Russians can raise their voices, express indignation, and imply threats. This should be seen for what it actually is—theatrics—although it also reflects a propensity for power plays.

You can respond in two ways: you can allow the Russians to speak their piece, hear them out, enjoy the performance, and respond in a firm but calm manner, or you can elect to talk tough yourself, which Russians will understand and respect as an indication of resolve and determination. Because he did not understand this, President John F. Kennedy gave Premier Nikita Khrushchev the impression, when they met in Vienna in 1961, that he was weak and could be intimidated by the emplacement of Soviet missiles in Cuba.

In most negotiations Russians maintain strict discipline and speak with one voice, that of their delegation chairperson. An exception to this rule may be found in commercial or other negotiations, where several government ministries or agencies are represented on the Russian side along with end users. Americans, by contrast, tend to speak with many voices, reflecting the pluralism of U.S. society as well as disparate views within the delegation. This confuses Russians because they do not know which American is speaking with authority, and they will be quick to exploit any perceived differences.

The most difficult part of a negotiation, Americans often report, is reaching agreement among the various viewpoints and interests of their own side. Any such differences should be resolved in advance, and Americans should speak with one voice at the negotiating table, remembering their national motto, *E pluribus unum.*

The choice of the language used may become an issue. Russians will usually request that official negotiations, or at least plenary sessions (with full delegations), be conducted in two languages, Russian and English, even when the Russian negotiators speak English well. Russians regard their language as a world language on a par with English. The French and many others do the same. In small working groups, however, negotiations may be held in English.

One or more members of the U.S. delegation should be designated note takers. Not everything that is said will have to be recorded, but it will prove useful to have a written record, particularly on issues that are unresolved. A note taker who knows Russian will have two advantages. First, all Russian statements will be heard twice, once in the original Russian and again in English translation, thus giving the note taker more time to write and to be certain that what is recorded is correct. Second, nuances in Russian may not come through in the English translation.

When speaking through an interpreter, use simple words, short phrases, and no colloquial expressions. Pause frequently and signal to the interpreter when to proceed. Show signs of listening attentively to your Russian interlocutor, even if you do not understand what is said, and don't interrupt. Look at the speaker, not the interpreter. And don't preface your remarks with "Tell him that. . . ." Speak directly to your interlocutor, not to the interpreter.

Interpreters vary in quality and consistency in both countries and can be a source of misunderstanding. It is always helpful to have someone on the U.S. side of the table who is conversant in Russian and can monitor the interpreting.

Patience is a Russian virtue that pays off in negotiations. When negotiating on home turf, Russians can afford to wait out the other side. For Americans, however, time is money, and Americans in Moscow may therefore be tempted to make concessions in order to reach agreement quickly and return home. Such temptations should be resisted. Conversely, Russians negotiating in the United States may wish to expedite an agreement, particularly if they are spending their own money for hotel and other costs.

Who goes first? Russians traditionally prefer to know the other side's position before giving their own. They may do this by accepting your draft in advance but pleading that their own is not yet ready to present in exchange. When Russians host a negotiation, they will usually invite the other side to speak first. There is no particular disadvantage in doing so if the general outline of what each side hopes to achieve is known, or if there is a unanimity of views in advance.

Surprises should be avoided. If some radically new idea is to be proposed, it would be best to discuss the proposal with the Russians informally in advance of the negotiations, thereby giving them time to study it and prepare a response. When presented with a new and unexpected proposal at the negotiating table, Russians will have to retreat to a previous position and seek instructions from higher up. And, as former U.S. ambassador to Moscow Llewellyn Thompson advised, "Don't maneuver the Russian bear into a corner from which there is no escape; in such a position he can become vicious."[178]

At the negotiating table the two drafts are compared line by line and word for word. Wherever the language of the Russian and English drafts is identical or similar in meaning, agreement is reached and those paragraphs are set aside. Where the two drafts differ in substance, brackets are placed around the language in question to signify the differences that remain to be negotiated. A Russian offer to negotiate and reach agreement on each article of the drafts seriatim (individually and in succession) should be politely declined. Instead, the two drafts should first be reviewed in their entirety to identify all differences before the actual negotiating begins. This will permit some bracketed passages to be traded off against others.

When Russians make a concession—accepting the language of the U.S. draft—they will usually expect a corresponding concession in return, a quid pro quo in another part of the draft. Where such tradeoffs occur, they should be of equal importance. Russians have been known to concede a minor point but then demand a major concession in exchange. To avoid this, agreement should be sought first on all minor differences between the two drafts. Major differences should be left to the final stage of the negotiation, the endgame.

Regarding concessions, negotiators should understand which side wants or needs the agreement more. That side, commonly referred to in French as the *demandeur,* would normally be expected to make more concessions.

Experienced negotiators will also include several "throwaways" in their draft. These are demands that they know in advance the other side cannot accept. At some stage of the negotiation these may be withdrawn in exchange for concessions by the other side, which will have its own throwaways.

THE ENDGAME

The Russian is patient until challenged.

—Russian proverb

The final stage of a negotiation, the endgame, is the most dramatic, similar to the final minutes of a close football game. The minor issues have been resolved, but one or more major differences are still outstanding. The score is tied, the clock is ticking, and one side or the other digs in for a goal-line stand.

Americans in such a situation, worn down by Russian patience and persistence, may be tempted to make concessions in order to end a lengthy negotiation and reach an agreement that may be better than no agreement at all. But if the issues in dispute are important, you should resist that temptation. It should be made clear that further concessions cannot be made and that it would be better to have no agreement than a poor one. In the endgame Russians can be firm, but when challenged they can also change positions radically if they want an agreement and are persuaded that the other side will not retreat.

When an impasse is reached, present your bottom line—your basic requirements that must be satisfied in order to agree. The Russians will appreciate this, but they will of course have their own bottom line. If there is to be an agreement, it must reflect the bottom lines of both sides.

In the endgame, agreement on differences can often be reached away from the negotiating table at a working lunch or during a break. The resolved issues should then be formally confirmed at the negotiating table. Russians are more difficult to draw out in a large forum with other Russians present. In a smaller group or, better still, one-on-one, they will often open up and reveal their innermost thoughts.

Russian negotiators may also have a personal, as well as an official, agenda. They may be concerned with promotion or demotion, personal advantage for themselves or their families, and the personal prestige resulting from a successful negotiation. If you can determine the nature of the negotiator's personal agenda, you will be better able to deal with it.

At times you may be able to agree to a particular point but may not be certain that the home office—government, board of directors, or financial backers—will also agree. In such cases, agreement can be reached *ad referendum*, meaning that it is contingent upon agreement by higher authorities. If you are visiting Moscow, you can usually accomplish this with a telephone call, fax, or e-mail to the home office. Bear in mind, though, that your telephonic communications may be monitored.

Beware of all-night sessions. To meet a deadline, there is often a temptation to continue negotiations through the night until an agreement has been hammered out. But such marathon meetings and the resulting fatigue can put undue pressure on one side or the other to capitulate or make concessions they may later regret. It's better to sleep on the differences and start anew and refreshed the following morning.

THE PAPERWORK

Don't brag about the deal until you get the seal.

—Russian proverb

Russians like to put agreements on paper, even on minor matters, duly signed by both parties, stating what has been agreed to and how it will be carried out. Even when a formal agreement has not been reached, Russians will want to sign a *protokol,* a joint statement or memorandum of understanding that records what has been discussed. The protokol is the Russian way, and it is almost impossible to avoid. Americans may wonder why they should sign something if no agreement has been reached. The protokol, however, can serve a useful purpose, for both sides, by providing a written record of what was discussed, what was agreed to, and what was not agreed to. For the Americans, it also demonstrates to the Russians that the Americans negotiated in good faith. The Russians may also need a protokol to present to their higher-ups when they argue in favor of the agreement. Don't be afraid to sign one— the protokol has no legal force—but make sure you know what it says.

When agreement has finally been reached on all major issues, there is still much to be done. First, there is the usual cleanup work—small differences of substance in the English and Russian versions of the agreement usually turn up and must be smoothed out. Second, the English and Russian versions of the agreed language must be reconciled.

Agreements customarily are signed in two versions, English and Russian, both equally valid. But to do this, someone on the American side who is fluent in Russian must sit down with a Russian who is fluent in English and compare the two language versions to verify that what they say and mean is identical. This is not easily done because, as we have seen, there are many expressions in one language for which there are no exact equivalents in the other. Major language differences can often be reconciled by minor changes in one language or the other. Be sure to avoid, however, the papering over of differences by saying that Americans will understand what is meant in English and that Russians will understand what is meant in Russian. Where such differences are substantial, they will inevitably resurface during implementation of the agreement and become a source of discord between the two parties, when each side is sure to interpret any ambiguous language in its own favor.

As any lawyer will advise, read agreements before you sign them and make certain that all language in the agreement is understood. Everything should be crystal clear, including who pays for what, a subject of importance to both sides.

And, as lawyers will also advise, if the subject of the agreement is important or involves financial or legal obligations, have a lawyer review it before you sign, even if that means reaching agreement ad referendum, that is, initialing the document rather than signing it, and then signing it later after the review has been completed.

VERIFICATION

Trust, but verify.

—Ronald Reagan (after an old Russian proverb)

Can Russians be trusted to honor commitments? The prudent response to this question—and to many other questions about Russia—is "Yes, but. . . ."

According to Zbigniew Brzezinski, Anglo-Saxons and Russians have different concepts of trust:

> The Anglo-Saxons approach these issues like negotiated, legal agreements. It might be called a litigational approach. To the Russians, a commitment is binding as long as it is historically valid, so to speak. And its historical validity depends on the degree to which that commitment is either self-enforcing or still mutually advantageous. If it ceases to be self-enforcing or mutually advantageous, it obviously has lapsed.[179]

To ensure that an agreement is observed, it is prudent to include a provision for regular review of implementation. This usually takes the form of periodic meetings between the two sides, held alternately in each country, to review past performance and make plans for the future. If such meetings are held, the agreement is more likely to be observed and not allowed to atrophy. As Ronald Reagan, recalling an old Russian proverb, repeatedly reminded Mikhail Gorbachev during their summit meetings, "Trust, but verify."

Related to verification are accountability and reporting, particularly where the expenditure of funds is involved. Russians can be notoriously lax about accounting for expended funds and using them effectively, a problem recognized by Mikhail Gorbachev.

One of perestroika's best-known slogans was *khozraschot,* usually translated as "cost accounting." The intent, however, was cost effectiveness, particularly in determining the real costs of producing goods and services. After 60 years of a command economy in which production costs were subsidized by the state, Russians have little experience in determining profit or loss. Under khozraschot, the objective was to make Russian enterprises self-sufficient by basing the prices of produced goods on true costs.

A related problem is accountability of funds. American donors to Russian cultural and philanthropic institutions have reported difficulties in obtaining prompt and detailed reporting on how their funds are being expended. Some new Russian foundations have scoffed at the standard regulatory and accounting procedures required by American donors. As one Russian foundation official put it, "We are all fine Christian men, and our [Russian] donors don't question what we do with their money."[180]

Such a response should not be seen as an intent to deceive but rather as an intercultural difference. Americans understand the need for accountability, annual financial reports, and audits by certified public accountants. But requesting such procedures from Russians may be seen as questioning their good faith and honesty. When encountering indignation over reporting requirements, Americans may wish to emulate Ronald Reagan by responding, "Trust, but verify."

EXPECT THE UNEXPECTED

Russia is predictable in the sense that it will continue to be unpredictable.

—Marshall Goldman

Things seldom go as planned with Russians. The will is there in most cases, but the bureaucracy is notoriously inefficient and its wheels turn slowly. A government that claims to give high priority to planning often inexplicably does things at the last minute and without a plan. And the best-laid plans may not be carried out as intended, even when details are spelled out in agreements that have been negotiated and signed in good faith.

"One of the most significant features of Russian behavior," wrote Wright Miller, an Englishman who lived in Russia for many years,

> [is] that abandonment to the thing in hand which makes it difficult for so many Russians to keep regular habits unless they are obliged, which makes them careless of detailed preparation . . . yet capable of bouts of long-continued activity which are beyond the endurance of the ordinary Westerner.[181]

Russians will often say, "In principle, it can be done." But in practice, it often cannot. Russians begin discussions with generalities and leave the details to be dealt with later. In their enthusiasm to reach agreement, officials may tend to exaggerate the possibilities by signing agreements and making promises that offer more than they are actually able to deliver.

Where should you start in picking up the pieces after an agreement has fallen apart? Throughout this book, much has been made of the importance of the personal factor in doing business in Russia, where people are often more important than machines or technology. For an agreement to be truly successful, there should be a personal relationship between an American on one side and a Russian on the other who both want to make something happen. When nothing happens—an agreement is not implemented—the American will have to return to the personal relationship. Reestablishing that relationship—by phone or preferably another visit—can help to make something happen.

And things do happen without planning, as President George H. W. Bush learned in May 1990 when Gorbachev, less than two weeks before his Washington summit meeting with Bush, unexpectedly made public his plans to also visit Minneapolis and California. The announcement created turmoil in the White House because the Kremlin had not presented an itinerary for the proposed coast-to-coast tour, hotel rooms had not been reserved in Minneapolis or California, and no provisions had been made for Gorbachev's security or for supplying the special fuel needed for his Aeroflot jet. As *The New York Times* noted, "even the most rudimentary preparations have not been made for the kind of cross-country trek that the White House would spend months planning."[182]

Failure to pin down details can also have unexpected consequences in cultural exchanges. The first U.S.-Soviet cultural agreement, signed in 1958, provided for "sister university" relationships between universities in the two countries. Under the agreement, Indiana University was paired with Tashkent University.

The following year, a delegation from Tashkent arrived in Bloomington, Indiana, without advance notice, on the Friday afternoon of a football weekend when all hotel and motel rooms had already been reserved. To make matters worse, the Soviets were without funds because they had flown from New York to Chicago and had then spent all their dollars for a taxi to Bloomington, *Illinois*—right city, wrong state. Moreover, the letter from Moscow announcing their arrival plans was received at the university after the delegation had completed its visit and returned home.[183]

Thirty years later, in 1989, hilarious history repeated itself. Five Russian chefs, in an exchange between U.S. and Russian food professionals, were lost for five hours in the New York City area. The Russians had landed at Newark Airport while their American hosts were awaiting them at Kennedy Airport, where they were expected to arrive. Nevertheless, the Russian and American chefs eventually found each other and were soon in the kitchen cooking things up together despite the misplaced and late arrival.[184]

Russians often don't comply with agreed-on timetables for action, and officials do not answer their mail promptly. The best way to finalize a decision or get a go-ahead is through a face-to-face meeting, which, of course, can mean a trip to Russia and an added expense.

But a trip to Novosibirsk once, for a face-to-face meeting, produced a surprise for one American from Minneapolis. After months of arranging his visit and confirming it by telex, the Twin Cities man traveled halfway around the world to meet a Russian fellow expert in the Siberian city, only to discover on arrival that his Russian colleague was in Minneapolis.[185] As explained by Susan Hartman, codirector of the Minneapolis group that arranged the Novosibirsk visit, "National organizations [in Russia] will disappear and reappear under different names with different people running them."[186] Americans, who are usually sticklers for planning, should be prepared to expect the unexpected.

Government policies are suddenly and inexplicably changed and new initiatives are announced without adequate preparation, as President Bill Clinton learned in Budapest in December 1994 at a 53-nation summit meeting on European security. At that meeting, Boris Yeltsin, after earlier agreeing to join NATO's Partnership for Peace, surprised the assembly by declaring Russia's open opposition to the expansion of NATO into Central and Eastern Europe, adding caustically that "Europe is in danger of plunging into a cold peace."[187] Four months later, Yeltsin's position changed again at his Moscow summit meeting with Clinton, where he agreed to Russia's joining the Partnership for Peace. And confirming Marshall Goldman's dictum about Russia's unpredictability, under Vladimir Putin as president the Russian position on NATO has shifted back and forth, between cooperation and open hostility.

What you *can* expect in meetings in Russia is traditional hospitality. The conference table will be laden with bottled water and soft drinks, cookies, and sweets, and tea or coffee will be served. When an agreement or contract is signed, the signatories can expect to raise a glass of champagne. A festive lunch or dinner for visitors will usually be held with the customary four courses—zakuski, soup, main course, and a dessert—and vodka and wine.

When Russians visit the United States, they expect the same treatment and are disappointed when their hospitality is not returned to the same degree. At the State Department, where funds for entertaining were negligible, we were always embarrassed when all we could offer our Russian visitors was coffee or tea in a Styrofoam cup. The Russians were initially impressed by the Styrofoam, which they had not seen before, but the novelty soon wore off. And be aware that when serving coffee or tea to Russians, it should always be served with something to eat, even if only a cookie.

SEVEN

Seeing the Real Russia

They occupy your every moment; they distract your thoughts; they engross your attention; they tyrannize over you by means of officious politeness; they inquire how you pass your days; they question you with an importunity known only to themselves, and by fete after fete they prevent you seeing their country.

—Marquis de Custine, *Empire of the Czar*

The Marquis de Custine's frustrations over Russian hospitality have been shared by many visitors since 1839. The Russian practice of keeping visitors occupied around the clock is an old one, and obsession with secrecy is often assumed to be the reason.

The KGB, to be sure, can still be expected to maintain its vigilance in protecting state secrets from the eyes of curious foreign visitors. But while society is now more open, Russian hosts may still persist in filling every available hour of a visitor's time with sightseeing and other activities.

The explanation lies in the seriousness with which Russians regard their obligations toward guests. *Gostepriimstvo* (hospitality) has a broader and deeper meaning in Russian than in English. In Russian it means overwhelming guests with food, drink, attention, and entertainment; total dedication to guests' every need and comfort; and making certain that they are not bored.

Unfortunately, such a busy schedule makes it more difficult for visitors to see the real Russia. Your visit to Russia should include more than a Kremlin tour, the circus, the Hermitage museum, and other obligatory tourist sights; you should try to learn how Russians live.

A department store is a good place to begin a city tour. Note the prices of the merchandise but don't attempt to convert the prices to dollars. Try instead to figure out what an item would cost a Russian in terms of a monthly wage. Wages have risen, along with inflation, but Russian acquaintances will know what the average worker currently earns; don't hesitate to ask.

Visit a food store and food markets to see what is available and note the prices. Check out the price of bread, a staple of the Russian diet. Flea markets, found in most cities, are also worth a visit; the biggest is Moscow's Sunday market in Ismailovo Park, but watch out for pickpockets.

Railroad stations are a scene out of old Russia. Each day millions of visitors swarm into Moscow, adding to the city's 11 million residents. Most of the visitors are on foraging trips from distances of up to a hundred miles to buy items that are not available in their hometowns. If you will visit only Moscow or another large city, those stations provide an opportunity to see common people from small towns and villages as well as the *bomzhi* (homeless) who are kept off the streets by the militsia. Also to be seen in railroad stations these days are many of the tens of thousands of homeless children—orphans or runaways from broken homes or dysfunctional families—who roam the streets of Moscow and other large cities, subsisting by begging and petty theft, and by getting handouts from soup kitchens and charitable organizations.

All of Moscow's railroad stations are accessible via the Metro. The Leningrad, Kazan, and Yaroslavl stations are conveniently located adjacent to each other at the Komsomolskaya Metro station. (Yes, in Moscow it's still called the Leningrad station.). But be cautious in buying food from street vendors, especially meat products and alcohol, which may not be good for your health.

The Metro is also a good place to "people watch," and while the fare has increased, it's still the best buy in town. With its more than 150 stations and a network of 150 miles, the Moscow Metro covers the city and is a model of efficiency. Moreover, travel underground is much faster than surface travel, as traffic jams can be massive and cause lengthy delays. The Metro carries 18 million passengers on an average work day and is very crowded during rush hours, but trains run every 90 seconds during rush hours, and every three to four minutes during the rest of the day. Tokens can be purchased for single trips and plastic cards for a number of trips. Route maps are available and will make the Metro easier to use.

Churches offer another glimpse of old Russia as well as an opportunity to see the growing interest in things Russian and spiritual. Of the 77,676

Russian Orthodox churches that existed before the Revolution, only a few thousand survived communist persecution. Many have now reopened and are well worth a visit.

Street crime, which rose sharply during the early 1990s, has now leveled off and is less than in many major U.S. cities. Nevertheless, foreigners are still targeted, and some precautions are advised. Don't call attention to yourself. Try not to stand out or look like a tourist. Leave expensive jewelry at home. Wear old clothes. Buy a Russian hat and wear it. Don't wear fancy shoes, a sure giveaway. Speak softly, try to blend in, and take the same precautions you would in New York City, Los Angeles, or London.

Beware of underground passages, which are often the scene of robberies. Protect yourself against pickpockets in crowds and in the Metro, as well as the bands of street urchins who surround tourists and deftly relieve them of their valuables. Wear a money belt and carry only small amounts of currency. Keep only what you need for that day in your pockets so you don't have to pull out a big wad of bills to make a purchase. If you give money to one beggar, you will soon be surrounded by many others with outstretched hands. And keep somewhere in a safe place a copy of the page in your passport with your photo, passport number, and date and place of issuance. It will expedite getting a replacement at your country's nearest consulate if your passport is lost or stolen.

Look down, not up, and watch your step. Russian streets can be full of potholes and other obstacles, and sidewalks have a habit of unexpectedly dropping off. And in winter, watch out for falling icicles, big enough to cause serious injury to pedestrians on the sidewalks below.

Traffic is supposed to stop for pedestrians but does not always do so, and drivers run red lights when they believe they can get away with it. Do not cross streets against traffic lights. Carry a small pocket flashlight at night. If you use taxis, negotiate the price before beginning your ride, and do not share rides with strangers. If traveling overnight by train, keep your compartment door locked and securely fastened. Keep your passport and visa with you at all times, in an inside pocket; the militsia makes checks for identity documents, and if you don't have yours, you may be fined or have to pay a bribe to be let off. Drink only bottled water, which is always available, and use it to brush your teeth.

But Moscow is not Russia. With its expanding middle class, shops with international names, monumental traffic jams, sushi bars, Internet cafes, and night life, Moscow has become much more European than the rest of Russia. Some compare it to New York.

The real Russia can be found in the many smaller cities, towns, and villages, where the bulk of the population lives, many of them in areas formerly closed to travel by foreign visitors. Those formerly closed cities, isolated for many years from the rest of the world because they were centers of military-industrial production, are more Russian. There the pace of life is slower, the people are more polite, and Western influence is less evident. In 1992, in Saratov, a large industrial city on the Volga River, I met with Russian teachers who taught English at the high school and university level, and they told me that I was the first native English speaker they had ever encountered. (It was a captive audience, and they hung on every word I uttered.) Such cities, now overcoming their previous isolation, are becoming increasingly important, politically and economically. And it is in the provinces that the real political pulse of Russia can be taken.

For a glimpse of old Russia, a village visit is also a must. The contrast between urban and rural life in Russia and America has been noted by writer Vassily Aksyonov:

> America's prosperity becomes apparent the moment you leave her large cities. In Russia the opposite is the case. What remains after the military has drained off most of the resources goes toward maintaining a minimal level of decency in the cities; the countryside and the villages are left to rot.[188]

EIGHT

Whither Russia?

Whenever the right of speech shall be restored to this muzzled people, the astonished world will hear so many disputes arise, that it will believe the confusion of Babel again returned.

—Marquis de Custine, *Empire of the Czar*

With free speech restored, the new Russia is indeed a Babel of disputes, as foreseen by the Marquis de Custine in 1839. But as Russians seek to develop a democracy and civil society, the disputes are far from civil and are better described as *skloka* (squabble).

"Skloka is a phenomenon born of our social order," wrote Olga Freidenberg, a cousin of famed writer Boris Pasternak. As she explained:

> Skloka stands for base, trivial hostility, unconscionable spite breeding petty intrigues, the vicious pitting of one clique against another. It thrives on calumny, informing, spying, scheming, slander, the igniting of base passions. . . . Skloka is the alpha and omega of our politics. Skloka is our method.[189]

In the early years of the twenty-first century, Russians are still squabbling. Absent a culture of compromise, everyone takes sides. Westernizers squabble with Slavophiles, liberals with conservatives, reformers with traditionalists, democrats with democrats, and communists with all of the above, and all of this takes place in a country with no tradition of political coalition building. The squabbling, moreover, is steeped with insults and abuse.

"In other countries," writes Pavel Palazchenko, Mikhail Gorbachev's former English interpreter and foreign policy aide, "people argue in order to find the truth. In this country you argue in order to prove that you are one hundred percent right and to destroy your opponent."[190] Or, as Gorbachev more politely put it, "we are an emotional people, we lack the culture to conduct debate and respect the viewpoint even of a friend, a comrade."[191]

Today's squabbling has roots in the Soviet past, claims Dmitri N. Shalin, a professor of sociology at the University of Nevada at Las Vegas:

> The emotional abuse that Russian intellectuals casually heap on each other these days is a sure sign that their predecessors were themselves abused. All those who had gone through Stalinist purges, were intimidated by the KGB, [and] witnessed ideologically inspired violence could not help being deeply troubled by their experiences.[192]

Indeed, the older generation is confused, frightened, less inclined to support change, and, with its nostalgia for the past, it is more likely to support the communists. Moreover, the confusion and fear is easily explained.

"Few nations," writes *The New York Times* correspondent Serge Schmemann, "have followed a historical trail quite as erratic, careening from feudalism to Brave New World, total war, famine, global might, and finally collapse, all in the span of one average lifetime."[193]

Less affected by this troubled past is the younger generation. Better educated than its elders, knowing more about Russia and the rest of the world, with access to the Internet, and with the optimism and energy of youth, they have greater hopes and expectations for the future. This generation is also more positive about the quality of their lives, with 64 percent claiming, in 2007, to be happy, compared with 46 percent in 1997, according to a study by the Sociology Institute of the Russian Academy of Sciences. However, the study also showed widespread apathy of young people aged 17 to 26 about elections, with 27 percent refusing to commit to a political party, 22 percent saying they did not vote, and 49 percent showing no interest at all in politics.[194]

A somewhat different view was shown by the late Yuri Levada, who was Russia's most respected pollster. According to Levada, 18- to 30-year-olds constitute the wealthiest and most dynamic demographic group in Russian society today:

> Out of all social groups, young people are the richest, the most well-off. They have bigger salaries and they don't have families yet or responsibilities. They know how to earn money and their salaries are the largest.

But, as Levada continued, in addition to their materialism and lack of interest in politics, young people also showed "a total absence of any larger ideas or values which you usually find in this segment of the population. They have no concept about any long-lasting values in life."[195]

That "burgeoning middle class," as it has been called, is unlike middle classes in the West. Like most other Russians, they show little or no interest in politics. More than half of them are employed by the state, either in government agencies or state-run corporations. They live for the present and do not plan for the future, and they spend rather than save. Content with their lives in a consumer society, they are unlikely supporters of change and have little interest in democracy.[196] Foreign travel and owning a new car and an apartment are of more importance to them. As *The Independent* put it, "Obtaining a mortgage [*ipoteka* in Russian] is the latest rite of passage for Russian professionals in pursuit of a middle-class lifestyle."[197]

Population decline is another of Russia's travails, with an astonishing 50 percent decline in births between 1987 and 1999. In most developed countries, population decline is due to a low birth rate, but Russia's low birth rate is combined with a high death rate. Mortality began to exceed births in 1992, and recent government efforts to correct the decline have been serious. Among other steps taken they include measures to reduce the easy access to abortions, and better care of newborns. Nevertheless, according to the Federal Service for State Statistics, by the end of 2025 the median variant estimate of the Russian population will be down to 135.6 million, a decrease of some 6 million from the population of 142 million on January 1, 2008.[198]

Life expectancy at birth has also declined. In 2006, it was 73.1 years for women and 60.56 for men. By comparison, life expectancy in the United States in 2000 was a record-high of 79.5 for women and 74.1 for men. In the United Kingdom, life expectancy in 2001 (estimated) was 80.6 for women, and 77.8 for men.

Particularly worrisome is the high death rate for people of working age. Half of Russian deaths in the 1990s were caused by cardiovascular diseases, with second place held not by cancer, as elsewhere in industrial countries, but by accidents and injuries as well as murders, suicides, and alcohol poisoning. These latter three factors were involved in half of all deaths among working-age men. As a result, the population of those of working age is predicted to fall by 13.6 million between 2005 and 2020.[199]

Contributing to these dire demographics are excessive use of alcohol and tobacco, poor nutrition, lower standards of sanitation, unhealthy working conditions and lifestyles, environmental degradation, deterioration of health care delivery systems, and a resultant return of infectious and other diseases. In recent years, Russia has suffered outbreaks of typhus, typhoid fever, and cholera. Drug-resistant tuberculosis has more than doubled since 1990. The incidence of syphilis has soared, and drug abuse has caused alarming increases in HIV/AIDS and hepatitis. Travelers to Russia should be sure that their immunizations are up to date and to mind their behavior.

HIV/AIDS has become a major problem in Russia. According to Vadim Pokrovsky, Russia's leading HIV/AIDS epidemiologist, the number of persons diagnosed in 2007 with full-blown AIDS—not HIV infections—rose by 54 percent from 2006, and during that same period the number of deaths from AIDS increased by 39 percent.[200] The rise in HIV/AIDS is attributed to government inaction and its failure to recognize what has become a crisis, said Richard Holbrooke, who heads the Global Business Coalition on HIV/AIDS, an alliance of 220 international corporations that promotes partnerships between governments and the private sector to combat HIV/AIDS and other infectious diseases. Holbrooke, a former U.S. ambassador to the United Nations, said that HIV/AIDS is spreading faster in Russia and Ukraine than anywhere else in the world, and 90 percent of HIV carriers in these countries will not know that they are infected until they get full-blown AIDS.[201]

Yet another troubling problem is the increase in road accidents, which has been termed "a national disaster" by Russia's interior minister. About one hundred people die every day in traffic accidents, with one-third of these involving pedestrians and cars. One of the causes is believed to be the growing number of automobiles on the road, which has been increasing each year by about one million.[202]

How can a developed country suffer such catastrophic demographic statistics? One simple but true answer is that life in Russia has always been cheap and short. Russian history has been replete with violence and human suffering—the Mongol conquest, wars with neighboring states, serfdom, pogroms, famines, immense loss of life in two world wars, the Red and White terrors of the civil war, Stalin's purges and the cruelties of the Gulag, the forced resettlement of ethnic groups, and the lawlessness and murders of present-day Russia.

But as the health of Russians has deteriorated, the health of the economy has improved as painful reforms have begun to show results. The high prices of crude oil, natural gas, and minerals provide much-needed foreign currency. A middle class is emerging, and the well being of many Russians has improved.

According to the Federal Statistical Service (*Rosstat*), direct foreign investment in Russia doubled to $27.8 billion from 2006 to 2007, and Russian investment abroad grew by 43.6 percent to $74.63 billion during that same period.[203]

Problems remain, however, with the manufacturing sector, where many industries are not competitive in international markets, but they cannot be closed because entire regions depend on them for employment and the services they provide to their employees. In 2005, an estimated 16 percent of the population lived below the poverty line, mostly those in rural areas and the elderly. Moreover, much of the Russian recovery, as well as its future, is based on the unpredictable price of oil and minerals on the world market.

As a consequence, the country remains divided between haves and have-nots, winners and losers in the privatization process. Among the haves is a phenomenon called "crony capitalism," in which interlocking networks of business and government officials, many with familiar faces from the communist nomenklatura, maintain monopolies and originate oligopolies. Among the have-nots are pensioners and others on fixed incomes who have been impoverished by inflation. Rampant crime affects both the haves and have-nots, and it is little wonder that many Russians, humiliated by their loss of empire and superpower status, are also embittered and demoralized by the decline in their living standard in so short a time span.

Yet, there is tranquility in the streets as Russians hunker down and endure, as they have done so often in the past. Food and consumer goods have become more expensive, but Russians no longer have to stand in long lines to make their purchases. And, as in the past, Russians have drawn on their agricultural heritage and are producing in their small private or communal gardens much of the food they consume.

As a result, many Russians are nostalgic for the economic stability and personal safety of the Brezhnev years. The longer a Russian lived under communism, the more likely he or she is to have clung to Soviet political values. A majority of the people regret the disintegration of the Soviet Union, but as the older generation has been dying the number of those regretting the breakup has declined. Over the course of 2007, this majority dropped from 61 to 55 percent, while proponents increased from 32 to 36 percent.[204]

A new leadership came to power in 2008, or is it the same leaders with new position titles? Vladimir Putin, having served his constitutional limit of two terms as president, is now prime minister. But Putin named as president the relatively unknown Dmitri Medvedev, chairman of the board of directors of *Gazprom*, the Russian energy giant, much as Boris Yeltsin had named the unknown Putin as his successor in 1999. And Medvedev was formally confirmed as president by an approval vote of 70.28 percent in the March 2008 elections.

Putin's progress, if that's what we may call it, has been criticized by many both at home and abroad. As *The Economist* put it in an editorial:

> Mr. Putin's slide into autocracy since he became Russia's president in December 1999 is well documented, as are his background in and his zealous promotion of the Russian secret service. In nearly eight years in the Kremlin he has crushed opposition, stripped regional governments of their autonomy, reasserted state control of Russia's energy resources and eliminated most independent media.[205]

However, Putin enjoys more than 70 percent popularity among Russia's public, which likes his energy, decision-making, character, and sobriety. And thanks to rising oil and other commodity prices, Russia's Gross Domestic Product (GDP) has been growing by 6 to 7 percent annually since 1999. Consequently, there is much national pride in a Russia that is once more to be reckoned with by the international community. But most important, to fulfill their longing for a "normal life" Russians now have a *vozhd* (strong leader) in the Kremlin and the *stabilnost* (stability) they so desired after the uncertainty and turbulence of the Yeltsin years.

Reforms are under way that are independent of current political leaders. Privatization is proceeding, although many of the former state-owned factories have been renationalized and are still run by the same directors and in the same way as in the past by their old managers, as well as with old machinery. As a Canadian economist comments:

> We know that it is difficult to change the behavior of managers in industry. Often it does not make much difference whether the enterprise is still state-owned, has been commercialized, or even really privatized. Despite changed objective conditions it is always easier to make decisions in the old familiar way. You have to "unlearn" the way the enterprises were run in the past in order to accept new criteria and methods.[206]

Russia has an elected president and parliament, and the parliament is independent although subordinate to the presidency. Voter turnout for elections—more than 60 percent—was higher than in the United States. A civil society is emerging in a country where, until recently, the government ran everything. Thousands of nongovernmental organizations have been registered by the Ministry of Justice and are providing assistance to millions of Russians. They represent independent civic action groups that work on such diverse issues as human rights, health, soldiers' rights, labor, small business, children's rights, anticonscription, women's rights, ethnicity, and many other causes that could not have been openly championed in the Soviet Union.

The new leadership team of Putin and Medvedev has many challenges, among which modernization is foremost if Russia wishes to remain a great power. But to modernize, to reduce its dependence on natural resources, and to overcome the handicaps inherited from the Soviet era, Russia needs the technology, know-how, and funding that can come only from the West. And for that, improved relations with the West, and especially with the United States, will be a requirement.

Crime and corruption are troublesome, and the pace and scope of reform may be questioned, but the process seems irreversible, although most informed observers believe it will take a generation or more to complete. But, as I have been writing since the first edition of this book in 1992, "whatever form of democracy emerges in Russia, history tells us that it will be based on many of the same forces that have shaped Russia in the past— geography, history, religion, culture, and governance. The new state will be neither European nor Asian, but uniquely Russian."[207] We should not expect it to be a replica of the democracy we know in the West.

AFTERWORD

Russia has often been too much for the Russians themselves—there has been just too much space, too much winter, too much suffering, too much bureaucracy, meanness, aspiration. It can certainly be too much for a visitor, no matter how sympathetic.

—Alfred Kazin, *Russian Sketches*

Human nature and national spirit cannot be changed overnight, especially by force. One can only hope to facilitate their internal processes.

—Fedor Burlatsky, "*War of Civilizations? Never!*"

RECOMMENDED READINGS

Åslund, Anders. 2002. *Building Capitalism: The Transformation of the Former Soviet Bloc.* New York: Cambridge University Press. The author, a well-known economist and former Swedish diplomat who formerly served as an adviser to Boris Yeltsin, shows in this comparative and intensively researched study what has and has not worked in Russia.

CIA World Factbook: Russia. A reliable reference tool with up-to-date facts and figures on Russia. https://*www.cia.gov/library/publications/the-world-factbook*

Collins, Naomi F. 2007. *Through Dark Days and White Nights: Four Decades Observing a Changing Russia.* Washington, DC: New Academia Publishing. A personal, eye-witness account of Russia from the mid-1960s through the turn of the twenty-first century, experiencing Russia through living there as a graduate student to life as the wife of the American ambassador.

Custine, Marquis de. 1989. *Empire of the Czar: A Journey Through Eternal Russia.* New York: Doubleday, Anchor Books. The Russia of 1839, as seen by a French traveler. Later travelers to Russia have marveled at how little has changed since Custine.

Department of State. *Background Note—Russia. www.state.gov/r/pa/ei/bgn/3183.htm.* Useful statistics on Russia.

English, Robert D. 2000. *Russia and the Idea of the West: Gorbachev, Intellectuals, and the End of the Cold War.* New York: Columbia University Press. How Soviet intellectuals turned the old thinking of the Stalin era into the new thinking that led to Gorbachev's glasnost, perestroika, and the end of the Cold War.

Feshbach, Murray. 2007. "Health Problems in Russian Power Structures: Present and Future Roles in Russian Politics," in Jan Leijonhielm and Fredrik Westerlund, eds. Stockholm: Swedish Defense Research Agency.

Gilbert, Martin. 1993. *Atlas of Russian History*, 2nd ed. New York: Oxford University Press. How Russia's boundaries have changed over the years.

Kohn, Hans, ed. 1955. *The Mind of Modern Russia.* New Brunswick, NJ: Rutgers University Press. Selected readings from great Russian writers and thinkers.

Riasanovsky, Nicholas V., and Mark Steinberg. 2004. *A History of Russia*, 7th ed. New York: Oxford University Press. Combining two volumes in one, this new and revised edition has proven popular.

Visson, Lynn. 1998. *Wedded Strangers:The Challenges of Russian-American Marriages.* New York: Hippocrene Books. A serious study of Russian-American marriages and the problems arising from the clash of two very different cultures, by an American woman who is married to a Russian.

ENDNOTES

1. Condoleezza Rice in an address at the State Department opening a conference on detente, October 23, 2007.
2. A senior Russian official in an interview with Baker and Glasser.
3. Peter Baker and Susan Glasser, *Kremlin Rising: Vladimir Putin's Russia and the End of Revolution* (New York: Scribner, 2005), 381.
4. As of this writing, the CIS loosely unites Armenia, Azerbaijan, Belarus, Georgia, Kazakhstan, Kyrgyzstan, Moldova, Russia, Tajikistan, Turkmenistan, Ukraine, and Uzbekistan.
5. François Guizot, quoted by Hans Kohn in *The Mind of Modern Russia* (New Brunswick, NJ: Rutgers University Press, 1955), vii.
6. A. P. Prokhorov, *Russkaya model' upravleniya* [The Russian Model of Management] (Moscow: Eksmo, 2006), 317.
7. Vikenty Matveyev, in a conversation with the author, Moscow, 1969.
8. Mikhail Gorbachev, in an address to the Parliamentary Assembly, Council of Europe, Strasbourg, France, July 6, 1989.
9. The Mongols were a Mongolian people; the Tatars were Turkic. But as the Mongol empire expanded, it encompassed more and more Turkic peoples. Hence, the Russian use of *Tatar* for *Mongol.*
10. In summer, by contrast, the days are long, and in the Russian north, it never gets dark at night. During St. Petersburg's Byeliye Nochi (White Nights), during the last two weeks of June, the sun barely dips below the horizon.
11. Karl Marx, quoted by Paul B. Henze in "Marx on Russians and Muslims," *Central Asian Survey* 6, no. 4 (1987), 36.
12. Richard Pipes, *U.S.-Soviet Relations in the Era of Détente* (Boulder, CO: Westview Press, 1981), 16.
13. Nicolas Zernov, *The Russians and Their Church* (Crestwood, NY: St. Vladimir's Seminary Press, 1978), 176. Zernov was a pioneer in the movement for Christian unity.
14. Nina Khrushcheva, "Culture Matters, But Not (of All Places) in Russia," in *Correspondence: An International Review of Culture and Society* (New York: Council on Foreign Relations, winter, 2000/2001 no. 7), 48.
15. The idea of land held in common for the benefit of the community has ancient roots in many societies. In England, it was customary before the Norman Conquest and the introduction of private property. One relic today, in the heart of an American city, is the Boston Common.

16. Richard Stites, *Revolutionary Dreams, Utopian Vision and Experimental Life in the Russian Revolution* (New York: Oxford University Press, 1989), 124.

17. Ibid., 207.

18. Related by Daniel Matuszewski, former IREX deputy director, in an e-mail to the author, December 15, 2001.

19. Lev A. Tikhomirov, *Russia, Political and Social,* quoted by Wright Miller in *Russians as People* (New York: E. P. Dutton, 1961), 81.

20. Laurens van der Post, *Journey into Russia* (Harmondsworth, England: Penguin Books, 1965), 173.

21. CIA World Factbook, July 2007. *https://www.cia.gov/library/publications/the-world-factbook/.*

22. Ibid.

23. These figures are from "International Religious Freedom Report 2006," issued by the Bureau of Democracy, Human Rights, and Labor, U.S. Department of State. For details, see *www.state.gov/g/drl/rls/irf/2006/71403.htm.*

24. James H. Billington, *The Icon and the Axe: An Interpretive History of Russian Culture* (New York: Random House, Vintage Books, 1970), 6.

25. Stites, *Revolutionary Dreams,* 16.

26. Paul Miliukov, in *Outline of Russian Culture, Part I, Religion and the Church,* edited by Michael Karpovich (New York: A. S. Barnes, 1960), 134.

27. Zernov, *The Russians and Their Church,* 182.

28. Ibid., 179.

29. Edward L. Keenan, in a lecture at the Kennan Institute, Washington, D.C., September 24, 1985, and in an interview with the author, March 22, 1991.

30. Nina Khrushcheva, "Culture Matters," 48.

31. Geoffrey Hosking, *The Awakening of the Soviet Union* (Cambridge: Harvard University Press, 1990), 132.

32. Ruth Amende Roosa, "Russian Industrialists Look to the Future: Thoughts on Economic Development, 1906–17," in *Essays in Russian and Soviet History,* John Shelton Curtiss, ed. (New York: Columbia University Press, 1963), 198–218.

33. Vladimir V. Belyakov and Walter J. Raymond, eds., *The Constitution of the Russian Federation* (Lawrenceville, VA: Brunswick Publishing, 1994), 27.

34. Much of the data on agriculture here has been drawn from Roy L. Prosterman, et al., *Russian Agrarian Reform: A Status Report from the Field* (Seattle: Rural Development Institute, August 1994).

35. "Background Note: Russia," U. S. State Department, February 2007.

36. Vladimir Shlapentokh, in Johnson's Russia List #114, May 20, 2007.

37. Marshall Shulman, in a Face-to-Face Lecture at the Carnegie Endowment for International Peace, Washington, DC, February 12, 1989.

38. Stephen F. Cohen, *Rethinking the Soviet Experience* (New York: Oxford University Press, 1985), 148.

39. *The New York Times,* June 1, 1990.

40. Andrew Jack, *Inside Putin's Russia* (London and New York: Oxford University Press, 2005), 62.

41. *RIA Novosti,* December 21, 2001.

42. Richard Lourie, *Predicting Russia's Future* (Knoxville, TN: Whittle Direct Books, 1991), 82.
43. Richard Lourie and Aleksei Mikhalev, "Why You'll Never Have Fun in Russian," *The New York Times Book Review* (June 18, 1989), 38.
44. Ibid., 38.
45. *The New York Times,* November 28, 1989.
46. Llewellyn Thompson, in his final briefing for American correspondents prior to his departure from Moscow in 1968, a meeting that the author attended.
47. Tibor Szamuely, *The Russian Tradition* (New York: McGraw-Hill, 1974), 6.
48. Aleksandr Oslon, in Johnson's Russia List #129, June 7, 2007.
49. George F. Kennan, *Memoirs,* 1925–1950 (Boston: Little, Brown, 1967), 528.
50. Ibid., 529.
51. Yevgeny Yevtushenko, *Literaturnaya Gazeta* (Moscow), April 7, 1958, quoted by Klaus Mehnert in *Soviet Man and His World* (New York: Frederick A. Praeger, 1961), 30.
52. Andrei Amalryk, *Notes of a Revolutionary,* translated by Guy Daniels (New York: Knopf, 1982), 271. Additional details are from an interview by the author with Alfred Friendly Jr., who heard the story firsthand from Amalryk.
53. Tatyana Tolstaya, "Notes from Underground," *The New York Review of Books 37,* translated by Jamey Gambrell (May 31, 1990), 4.
54. Ibid.
55. Ibid.
56. Irwin Weil, in an interview with the author, February 4, 1991.
57. Ibid.
58. Aleksandr Solzhenitsyn, *The Oak and the Calf: Sketches of Literary Life in the Soviet Union* (New York: Harper and Row, 1975), 497–98.
59. Marquis de Custine, *Empire of the Czar: A Journey Through Eternal Russia* (New York: Doubleday, Anchor Books, 1989), 183.
60. Russia's plan (not yet fully implemented) to reform the military includes cutting manpower by one-third, modernizing weapons, , abolishing the draft, and making the military a fully professional force.
61. Anton Chekhov, in *Three Sisters,* Act II.
62. Ronald Hingley, *The Russian Mind* (New York: Charles Scribner's Sons, 1977), 189.
63. *Constitution (Fundamental Law) of the Union of Soviet Socialist Republics* (Moscow: Novosti, 1977), 38.
64. Belyakov and Raymond, *The Constitution of the Russian Federation,* 22.
65. Statistics from Russia's State Statistics Committee, excerpted from "ITAR-TASS Reports Women Earn Less Than Men, Have Better Education" (Moscow, March 8, 2005).
66. Ibid.
67. Ibid.
68. Mikhail Gorbachev, *Perestroika: New Thinking for Our Country and the World* (New York: Harper & Row, 1987), 116–17.
69. Murray Feshbach, in "Russian Military: Population and Health Constraints," a paper prepared for the Conference on Russian Power Structures: Present and Future

Roles in Russian Politics, sponsored by the Swedish Research Institute of National Defense and the Swedish Defense Commission, Stockholm, October 17–18, 2007.

70. Feshbach, in a talk at the Kennan Institute, Washington, DC, November 1, 1994, and in a conversation with the author.

71. *Moscow Times,* November 29, 2001.

72. Women's Day was formerly known as International Women's Day.

73. Lynn Visson, *Wedded Strangers: The Challenges of Russian-American Marriages* (New York: Hippocrene Books, 1998).

74. Mikhail F. Antonov, quoted by Bill Keller, "Yearning for an Iron Hand," *The New York Times Magazine* (January 28, 1990), 19.

75. Serge Schmemann, in *The New York Times,* February 20, 1994.

76. *The New York Times,* January 30, 1991.

77. *The New York Times,* February 3, 2005.

78. *The Boston Globe,* January 26, 2001.

79. Yuri Levada, in *The San Francisco Chronicle,* February 14, 2001.

80. *The New York Times,* September 20, 2000.

81. Hugh Seton-Watson, *The Decline of Imperial Russia, 1855–1914* (New York: Frederick A. Praeger, 1952), 24.

82. *Time,* July 24, 1989, 61.

83. Georgi Poltavchenko, in *Rossiskaya Gazeta,* August 5, 2000.

84. Pyotr Savitsky, quoted by Françoise Thom in "Eurasianism: A New Russian Foreign Policy," *Uncaptive Minds* 7, no. 2 (Summer 1994), 66.

85. Tibor Vasko, "Some Thoughts on Transformation by a Retired System Practitioner," in Marie Lavigne, ed., *ALMANAC(H),* 105.

86. Robert G. Kaiser, in *Washington Post Book World,* July 8–14, 2001.

87. George Vernadsky, *The Mongols and Russia* (New Haven: Yale University Press, 1953), 337.

88. Yuri Afanasyev, "The Coming Dictatorship," in *The New York Review of Books* (January 31, 1991), 38.

89. George F. Kennan, "After the Cold War," *The New York Times Magazine* (February 5, 1989), 38.

90. *The New York Times,* March 23, 1991.

91. Ferdinand Protzman, "2 German-Soviet Pacts Called Vital First Steps," *The New York Times,* June 15, 1989.

92. *www.transparency.org/policy_research/surveys_indices/cpi/2007.*

93. Yves Gisse, "Valeurs culturelles traditionelles et transition économique," in *ALMANAC(H)* edited by Marie Lavigne (Pau, France: self-published, 1997), 307.

94. International Federation of Journalists, May 28, 2007.

95. Marshall Goldman, "Comrade Godfather," *The Washington Post,* February 12, 1995.

96. *The New York Times,* April 7, 1995.

97. Yevgenia Albats, in *Moscow Times,* December 20, 2001.

98. *The New York Times,* February 14, 1990.

99. Nikolai Berdiaev, *The Origin of Russian Communism* (Ann Arbor: University of Michigan Press, 1960), 113.

100. Nicholas P. Vakar, *The Taproot of Soviet Society* (New York: Harper and Brothers, 1962), 75.

101. Richard S. Wortman, *The Development of a Russian Legal Consciousness* (Chicago: University of Chicago Press, 1976), 3.

102. Nikita Khrushchev, quoted by Konstantin M. Simis, *USSR: The Corrupt Society* (New York: Simon & Schuster, 1982), 29–31.

103. Harold J. Berman, *Justice in the U.S.S.R.,* rev. ed. (Cambridge: Harvard University Press, 1963), 191–93, and in correspondence with the author.

104. Ibid., 222.

105. Ibid., 270.

106. Khrushcheva, *Culture Matters,* 48.

107. In this treatment of judicial reform, the author has drawn from Peter H. Solomon Jr., *Fixing Courts in Russia? The Putin/Kozak Reforms of 2001* (Cambridge, MA: Cambridge Energy Research Associates, Inc., 2001).

108. Ibid.

109. Ibid.

110. See Eugene Huskey, "Lowering the Barriers to Entry for Russian Small Business," in Kathryn Hendley, ed., *Remaking the Role of Law: Commercial Law in Russia and the CIS* (New York: Juris Publishing, 2007).

111. Richard Marsland, "At Risk of Losing a Wild Reputation: Russia," *Financial Times* (London), April 4, 2001.

112. Ibid.

113. Peter H. Solomon Jr., "Bias and Political Influence in Russian Courts," unpublished memo, January 2007.

114. Ibid.

115. A U.S. lawyer with many years of experience in Russian courts.

116. Alexander Rahr, *Wladimir Putin: Der Deutsche im Kreml* (Muenchen: Universitas, 2000).

117. Martin Malia, "What Is the Intelligentsia?" in *The Russian Intelligentsia,* Richard Pipes, ed. (New York: Columbia University Press, 1961), 7.

118. Hingley, *The Russian Mind,* 207.

119. Custine, *Empire of the Czar,* 496.

120. V. I. Lenin, *Selected Works 9* (New York: International Publishers, 1943), 356.

121. *The New York Times,* August 20, 1990.

122. *The Washington Post,* October 28, 1994.

123. Serge Schmemann, in *The New York Times,* February 20, 1994.

124. In *Crossroads,* newsletter of the American Collegiate Consortium for East-West Cultural and Academic Exchange, Middlebury, VT (Spring 1991).

125. Landon Pearson, *Children of Glasnost: Growing Up Soviet* (Seattle: University of Washington Press, 1990), 94.

126. Susan Jacoby, *Inside Soviet Schools* (New York: Hill and Wang, 1974).

127. Pearson, *Children of Glasnost,* 93.

128. Ibid, 111–12.

129. *The Washington Post,* September 18, 1995.

130. See Ben Eklof and Edward Dneprov, Eds., *Democracy in the Russian School: The Reform Movement in Education Since 1984* (Boulder, CO: Westview Press, 1993), 3–4.

131. See *http://english.pravda.ru/society/stories/98271-1/.*

132. More than half of all students in higher education now pay fees.

133. Johnson's Russia List #223, October 27, 2007.

134. Stites, *Revolutionary Dreams,* 244.

135. Inge Morath and Arthur Miller, *In Russia* (New York: Viking, 1969), 15.

136. Hingley, *The Russian Mind,* 179.

137. Stites, *Revolutionary Dreams,* 244–45.

138. *The New York Times,* July 19, 1989.

139. Mikhail Heller and Aleksandr M. Nekrich, *Utopia in Power, The History of the Soviet Union from 1917 to the Present,* translated by Phyllis B. Carlos (New York: Summit Books, 1986), 508.

140. William McCulloch, in a lecture at the Kennan Institute, Washington, DC, March 14, 1994.

141. *Parade Magazine* (October 8, 1989), 27.

142. If you find this strange, pick up your local telephone directory and see how many Johnsons (son of John) and Andersons (son of Andrew) are listed. This helps distinguish familial relationships.

143. Morath and Miller, *In Russia,* 15.

144. Nina Belyaeva, quoted by Georgie Anne Geyer, ". . . wrong basket?" *The Washington Times,* May 31, 1990.

145. Stites, in an interview with the author, February 11, 1991.

146. Hosking, *Awakening of the Soviet Union,* 13.

147. Johnson's Russia List #118, May 24, 2007.

148. Vaclav Havel, in his acceptance speech on receiving the German Booksellers Association's Peace Prize, October 15, 1989, translated by A. G. Brain, *The New York Review of Books* (January 18, 1990), 8.

149. Custine, *Empire of the Czar,* 437.

150. Andrei Sinyavsky [Abram Tertz, pseud.], "Thought Unaware." *New Leader 48,* no. 15 (July 19, 1965), 1.

151. Hedrick Smith, *The Russians* (New York: Times Books, Quadrangle, 1976), 120–21.

152. In Anna Hunt, "So Has the Russian Mafia Met Its Match?" *The Independent* (UK), November 2001.

153. *The New York Times,* November 7, 2007.

154. Marshall I. Goldman, "Gorbachev at Risk," *World Monitor* (June 1990), 38.

155. Johnson's Russia List #20, January 29, 2008.

156. Johnson's Russia List #25, February 5, 2008. According to official sources, in 2006 there were 42,855 suicides in Russia, and the rate in January 2008 was 30 suicides per 100,000 people a year, which put Russia in second place in the world for suicide rates (Lithuania ranks the highest).

157. Johnson's Russia List #20, January 29, 2008.

158. For this quote, as well as other material on vranyo, I am indebted to Hingley, *The Russian Mind,* 91, and Hingley, "That's No Lie, Comrade," *Problems of Communism 11,* no. 2 (1962), 47–55.

159. Boris Fedorov, in *The Washington Post,* May 1, 2001.

160. Fyodor Dostoyevsky, "A Word or Two about Vranyo," *Diary of a Writer,* quoted by Hingley in *The Russian Mind,* 105.

161. Hingley, "That's No Lie," 54.

162. *The New York Times,* May 11, 1995.
163. I have drawn here from a Reuters dispatch from Moscow, reported in Johnson's Russia List #4467, August 21, 2000.
164. E-mail from John Schillinger, University of Maryland, November 8, 2007.
165. Furman Nelly, David Goldberg, and Natalia Lusin, "Enrollments in Languages Other Than English in United States Institutions of Higher Education, Fall 2007," New York: Modern Language Association, November 2007.
166. Johnson's Russia List #229, November 5, 2007.
167. Hingley, *The Russian Mind,* 206.
168. Lourie and Mikhalev, "Why You'll Never Have Fun in Russian," 38.
169. Kornei Chukovsky, *The Art of Translation,* translated by Lauren G. Leighton (Knoxville: University of Tennessee Press, 1984), 11–12.
170. Lyudmila Putin, quoted in "Ljudmila staunt," *Der Spiegel* (Germany), (February 19, 2001).
171. David Remnick, "The Trial of the Old Regime," in *The New Yorker* (November 30, 1992), 120.
172. Barbara Monahan, *A Dictionary of Russian Gesture* (Tenafly, NJ: Hermitage, 1983), 15.
173. George F. Kennan, *Memoirs, 1925–1950* (Boston: Little, Brown, 1967), 564.
174. *The New York Times,* February 25, 2001.
175. Albertas Laurinciukas, "How I Failed to Find the Average American," *Soviet Writers Look at America,* edited by Alexander Fursenko (Moscow: Progress Publishers, 1977), 175.
176. Sir William Hayter, *The Kremlin and the Embassy* (London: Hodder and Stoughton, 1966), 133.
177. Eliza K. Klose, in *Surviving Together 12* (Autumn 1994), 2.
178. Llewellyn Thompson, in his final briefing for American correspondents prior to his departure from Moscow in 1968, a meeting that the author attended.
179. Zbigniew Brzezinski, in an interview with Radio Liberty-Radio Free Europe, quoted in *The Wall Street Journal,* March 25, 1983.
180. Sharon Tennison, Center for U.S.-U.S.S.R. Initiatives, San Francisco, California, in a memo to U.S. foundations, May 15, 1990.
181. Wright Miller, *Russians as People,* 90.
182. *The New York Times,* May 20, 1990.
183. Robert F. Byrnes, *Soviet-American Academic Exchanges, 1958–1975* (Bloomington: Indiana University Press, 1976), 62–63.
184. Marian Burros, "5 Russians Skirmish with a U.S. Kitchen and Everyone Wins," *The New York Times,* July 19, 1989.
185. *The New York Times,* May 28, 1990.
186. Ibid.
187. *The New York Times,* December 6, 1994.
188. Vassily Aksyonov, *In Search of Melancholy Baby,* translated by Michael Henry Heim and Antonina W. Bouis (New York: Random House, Vintage Books, 1989), 30.
189. Olga Freidenberg, in Elliot Mossman, ed., *The Correspondence of Boris Pasternak and Olga Freidenberg, 1910–1954* (New York: Harcourt Brace Jovanovitch, 1982), 303–04.

190. Pavel Palazchenko, *My Years with Gorbachev and Shevardnadze: The Memoir of a Soviet Interpreter* (University Park: Pennsylvania State University Press, 1997), 153.

191. Mikhail Gorbachev, in a speech to cultural and media executives, in Pravda, July 15, 1987.

192. Dmitri N. Shalin, "Intellectual Culture," in Dmitri N. Shalin, ed., *Russian Culture at the Crossroads: Paradoxes of Post-Communist Consciousness* (Boulder, CO and London: Westview Press, 1995).

193. Serge Schmemann, in *The New York Times,* December 26, 1993.

194. *Moscow Times,* June 5, 2007. Also, Johnson's Russia List #127, June 5, 2007.

195. Yuri Levada, quoted in Jeremy Bransten, "Russia: Nation's Youth Are Apolitical and Materialistic" (Moscow: RFE/RL), November 7, 2001.

196. See Masha Lipman, "Russia's Apolitical Middle," *The Washington Post,* June 4, 2007.

197. "Surge in Home Ownership," *The Independent* (UK); Johnson's Russia List #202, September 26, 2007.

198. *Demographic Yearbook of Russia, Official Edition* (Moscow: Federal State Statistics Service, 2007), 527–28.

199. Murray Feshbach, "Russian Military: Population and Health Constraints," a paper at the Conference on Russian Power Structures: Present and Future Roles in Russian Politics, Stockholm, October 17–18, 2007.

200. Feshbach, "Russian Military."

201. Johnson's Russia List #223, October 27, 2007.

202. Johnson's Russia List #224, October 29, 2007.

203. Johnson's Russia List #40, February 25, 2008.

204. Levada Analytical Center, reported by Interfax, December 24, 2007; Johnson's Russia List #263, December 26, 2007.

205. *The Economist* (October 6–12, 2007).

206. Zbigniew M. Fallenbuchl, "'Unlearning' and the Process of Transition," in *ALMANAC(H),* 48.

207. Yale Richmond, *From Nyet to Da: Understanding the Russians* (Yarmouth, ME: Intercultural Press, 1992), 161.

INDEX

abortion, 48
absolutism, 59–60
accountability, 134–135
acquisitiveness, 93
Aeroflot, 44
Afanasyev, Yuri, 60
agriculture, 13
    arable land and, 33
    collective farms, 14–15
    egalitarianism and,
        30–33
    entrepreneurs in, 31–32
    mir, 13–14
Aksyonov, Vassily, 142
alcoholism, 103–106,
    145–146
Amalryk, Andrei, 40
Andreyev, Leonid, 106
anti-Semitism, 21, 26–27,
    52
Antonov, Mikhail F., 51
apathy, 144, 145
applause, 111
artels, 13–14
arts, 40, 45–46
astrology, 23, 35–36
atheism, 25
authority, xx, 53, 80
    education and, 84, 88
autonomous entities,
        Russian Federation, 18
autonomy movements, 18

Baikal-Amur Railway,
    opening of, 109
Baker, Peter, xiv
Baltic republics, 19–20
Baryshnikov, Mikhail, 96
Belarus, 18, 19, 55–56
Belyaeva, Nina, 98
Berdyaev, Nikolai, 29, 43,
    72
Berman, Harold J., 73

big is beautiful, xx, 43–45,
    123
Billington, James, 23
birth control, 48
birth rate, 17, 145–146
blackmail, 70–71
Blaney, John, 62
blat (influence), 65
body language, 16, 118
Bologna Convention, 88
brain drain, 37
Brezhnev, Leonid, 8, 16, 23
bribes, 64, 65–66, 87
Brzezinski, Zbigniew, 134
Buddhists, 22
bureaucracy, 61–65
Bush, George H. W., 34, 51,
    136
Bush, George W., 51–52
business cards, 97–98
Byzantium, 23–24

candidness, 109
capitalism, crony, 147
Carter, Jimmy, 16
Catherine the Great, 109
Catholic Church, 22
Chechnya, ethnic
    consciousness in, 18
Chekhov, Anton, 45
Chernomyrdin, Viktor, 35
chess, 126
children. See family
China, comparing Russia
    with, 10
Chukovsky, Kornei, 116
churches, 140–141
Churchill, Winston, 61
cities. See urbanization
climate, 7–9
Clinton, Bill, 137
clothing, 110–111
cocktail parties, 105

Cohen, Stephen F., 34
Cold War, xiii, xiv
collectivization of farms,
    14–15
colleges and universities, 85,
    86–89
colossalism, xx, 43–45, 123
commerce
    alcoholism and, 105
    distances and, 10
    egalitarianism and, 31
    legal system and, 77–79
    mercantilism and, 11–12
    social factors in, 94–98
    women in, 49–50
Commonwealth of
    Independent States
    (CIS), 19–20
communalism, xx, 12–17,
    155n15
    individualism vs., 15–16
    in the law, 74
communication
    being candid in, 109,
        119
    caution in, 70–71
    forms of address and, 97
    language and, 113–115
    lies/fibs in, 106–109
    mail, 137
    misunderstandings in,
        116–117
    style differences in,
        117–119
    telephone, 119–121
    toasts and, 101–103
Communist Party
    religion under, 25
    women in, 46
compromise, 72
Connell, Rachel, 82
consensus building, 27, 72
conservatism, 33–35, 48